STAND RIGHT AND PRAY

Life-Transforming,
Nation-Shaking Prayer

DAYNE MASSEY

Stand Right and Pray

Trilogy Christian Publishers A Wholly Owned Subsidiary of Trinity Broadcasting Network

2442 Michelle Drive Tustin, CA 92780

Manufactured in the United States of America

10 9 8 7 6 5 4 3 2 1

Library of Congress Cataloging-in-Publication Data is available.

ISBN 978-1-63769-320-9

ISBN 978-1-63769-321-6

DEDICATION

This book is dedicated to all those who prayed for me through the years. My life would not be what it is today without your prayers. First, to my mother, Kathleen. Your prayers for me that my life would be Christ-centered are what caused me to surrender to Jesus and to pursue the call of God. To my grandmother, Ann Brackin. You have not ceased to pray for me that I would stand in the perfect will of the Father. Even as I write this book, at ninety-six years of age, you still pray for me unceasingly. To my wife, Lisa. We have walked together and developed in prayer together. You have been willing to go anywhere and to do anything in order to follow God's plan for our lives. I love you for who you are! To my daughter, Lydia. To see you passionate about Jesus is the joy of my heart. May your life of prayer far exceed anything that I have ever known and experienced. This book is also dedicated to the life and ministry of Kenneth E. Hagin, who taught me so much about prayer, by both precept and example.

INTRODUCTION

Posture is everything when it comes to prayer. Not your physical posture, like kneeling, standing, or sitting, but your spiritual posture. How you position yourself before Jehovah God. Many position themselves before God as an unworthy servant. Their prayers sound more like begging and pleading. Many people, as they attempt to pray, see themselves as sinful people who have no confident audience with the Father. Others may see themselves under the weight of rules and regulations that they have to keep and maintain in order to gain an audience with God.

This book is written with one main goal in mind...to teach the reader how to posture themselves correctly, according to New Testament scripture and to stand right and pray. Not to stand in one's own righteousness, but in the righteousness that has been given to us in Christ. Without understanding the subject of righteousness, and letting that righteousness be the foundation that we pray from, we will pray with a mixture of old covenant ways and new covenant ways. Old covenant ways are based on your own standing and your ability to keep the law. New covenant praying is praying in line with the finished work of Jesus.

We are not under the law, but we are under a new covenant of grace. You must know the difference when it comes to living for God, and you must know the difference when it comes to prayer. We live in the new! The only effective life of prayer is a prayer life that is based on the finished work of Jesus Christ. When we pray "in Jesus' name," what we mean is we are praying as Jesus would pray. We stand in His place of sonship and His righteousness and we pray with those kind of credentials. We pray with His standing and His qualifications because we stand in Christ!

Prayer is like the art of romance…everyone does it, but few are very good at it! To be good at prayer requires an understanding of the scriptures, an understanding of the difference between the old covenant and the new covenant, but also requires experience. Putting what you learn into practice and learning as you go. It's like driving a car. You can learn things about driving a car by reading manuals and textbooks, but you will never really learn how to drive a car until you get behind the steering wheel and begin to put all those truths about driving into practice.

This book will not help you unless you use it as a guide to practice praying. You will learn many wonderful truths here in this book, but to learn to pray effectively you must begin to effectively pray. Pray before you read this book and ask the Lord for greater understanding of prayer. Pray while you are reading this book by pausing and taking the time to put in practice what you read. Pray after you read each chapter.

Introduction

Like most everything in life, prayer is something that is built on a strong foundation. Perhaps you already have a strong foundation of new covenant praying. If so, this book will inspire you to continue to build a strong, effective life of prayer. Maybe your foundation for prayer was laid using a lot of tradition and not scriptural truth. If that is the case, then this book will help you break up the tradition that is causing your prayer life to be ineffective, and lay new foundations that you can build a life of prayer on that will cause what you pray to actually come to pass. Perhaps you are brand new at praying. Then you are in a perfect place to begin to establish your prayer life on the Word of God and truly become effective at seeing transformation in your live and the lives around you.

Prayers should be answered, and they will be if they are prayed according to God's will and His plan. Prayer should be transformational personally in the life of the one who is praying, and also in the lives of the ones that you pray for. Prayer should also be nation-shaking! Our prayers give God the invitation to come and do what He wants to do in our nation, and in the world. Are you ready to see life-transforming prayer? Are you ready to pray nation-shaking prayers that drive back the forces of evil and establish God's kingdom in the earth? Get ready! It is time to stand right and pray!

TABLE OF CONTENTS

GOD'S INVITATION TO PRAY

Why Does God Need Us To Pray?

Millions have used the phrase, "God is in control," but have you ever really thought deeply about that statement? Is God really in control? Is He controlling thieves and murderers? Is He controlling catastrophic storms that take hundreds and thousands of lives? Is He in control where starvation exists? What about where evil regimes of government take the lives of innocent people and endeavor to control with fear?

If God has everything in control and He is somehow secretly behind everything that happens, then why pray? Why not just leave God alone to perform His mysterious, sovereign wonders? The truth is God is not in control because He chose the world to function in a different way. The founder of the Wesleyan and the Methodist movement, John Wesley, once said, "It seems that God will do nothing unless a man prays. Why this is, we do not know."

Well, if this statement made by Wesley is true, then we ought to know why it is true! Is there a truth from God's word that shows us why we must pray, and why God is withholding things until we pray? Is the invitation from God to pray not one of just pleasure of intimacy with our creator, but one of necessity if we want help from the Almighty? Could it be that God is waiting on us, while many think they are waiting on Him? Let's dive into His word and find out!

Authority: God's Original Intent

Psalm 8 is a very peculiar psalm. It is as if someone is beholding God's amazing creation, and then he notices something strange about God's behavior toward one of His creatures...man.

> *What is man that You are mindful of him, and the son of man that You visit him? For You have made him a little lower than the angels, and You have crowned him with glory and honor. You have made him to have dominion over the works of Your hands; You have put all things under his feet, All sheep and oxen—Even the beasts of the field, The birds of the air, and the fish of the sea that pass through the paths of the seas. O Lord, our Lord, how excellent is Your name in all the earth!*

Psalm 8:4–9

Man is different than any other part of creation. The writer of the psalm noticed that man, above all other creatures, had God's attention. He was special, and God's purpose for man was to be the ruler of the earth. God had put all things under his dominion, and nothing had more power, more authority, and more responsibility than man did.

One amazing part of this psalm is in verse five, when it says that God has made man a little lower than the "angels." The Hebrew word from which "angels" is translated from, is not the word for angels at all. It's the Hebrew word *elohim*, which is the plural tense for God Himself. It's the same word used in Genesis when God said "Let *us* make man in *our* image. The passage in Psalm 8:5 should read "Thou hast made him a little lower than Yourself."

Angels are actually lower than man in rank and authority. Hebrews 1:14 states, *"Are they not all ministering spirits sent forth to minister for those who will inherit salvation?"*

Who are the heirs of salvation? We are! So angels minister for us and to us much like a servant does. Psalm 103:20 says, *"Bless the LORD, you His angels, who excel in strength, who do His word, heeding the voice of His word."* One purpose that angels have is to perform the words of God. When God's word is spoken by Him, or by one that He has put in authority, angels work to bring that word to pass.

We see this about angels again in the book of Revelation when the apostle John finds himself standing before an angelic being. Caught up in the awe of the presence of this great being, John falls down and begins to worship the angel. Listen to the angels response:

And I fell at his feet to worship him. But he said to

me, "See that you do not do that! I am your fellow servant, and of your brethren who have the testimony of Jesus. Worship God! For the testimony of Jesus is the spirit of prophecy."

Revelation 19:10

So, you see angels were not created to be above man, but to serve man in the work of God. When a man declares the words of God with the authority that God has given him, angels go to work to bring God's words to pass. Man is created a little lower than God Himself. But why you might ask? This psalm, along with many other scriptures, tells us that He intended for us to rule the earth as an ambassador, or as His co-regent.

We find from the very beginning of creation that God's original intention for His man was for him to rule the earth under God's umbrella of authority. Take a look at Genesis 3 and notice the words in bold:

*Then God said, "Let Us make man in Our image, according to Our likeness; **let them have dominion** over the fish of the sea, over the birds of the air, and over the cattle, over all the earth and over every creeping thing that creeps on the earth." So God created man in His own image; in the image of God He created him; male and female He created them. Then*

14

*God blessed them, and God said to them, "Be fruit-ful and multiply; fill the earth **and subdue it; have dominion** over the fish of the sea, over the birds of the air, and over every living thing that moves on the earth."*

Genesis 1:26–28

God created this earth for man. He created the place where man would rule and provided everything man would ever need before He set man here. God has chosen for the heavens to be His place of dominion, but He has chosen to give the earth to man.

"The heaven, even the heavens, are the LORD's; But the earth He has given to the children of men" (Ps. 115:16).

This explains a lot! First, it explains why bad things happen to good people. If God has put us in control, then we must pray and use our God-given authority. God doesn't help the good people and reject the bad. Jesus said that God causes the sun to rise on the good and the evil, meaning He is good to all. A lack of knowledge of the authority you have been given can cause you to perish. A lack of knowing how to pray effectively can limit your authority in the earth.

Second, it explains why Jesus had to come as a man. A man (by Adam's sin) got this earth in a mess, and a man had to straighten it out, all because God delegated His authority to man. Jesus had to be born a man. He had to accomplish everything as a man, trusting in God's ability to empower

Him to achieve everything He did. Adam caused man to fall from the glory of his created purpose of being a ruler.

"For all have sinned and fall short of the glory of God" (Rom. 3:23).

Jesus came to restore us to that place of fellowship and intimacy with the Father. Jesus also came to restore man's God-given dominion and authority that Adam relinquished to Satan when he sinned.

"For it was fitting for Him, for whom are all things and by whom are all things, in bringing many sons to glory, to make the captain of their salvation perfect through sufferings" (Heb. 2:10).

Now, because of Jesus' finished work, (His death, burial, resurrection, ascension and seating at God's right hand), we can advance God's kingdom with power and authority through prayer. We can pray and see God's will done in the earth, no matter what is happening, and no matter who seems to be endeavoring to stop God's plan!

Partnering With God

God is inviting us to come into this powerful place of partnering with Him in His work. We cannot do it without Him...He will not do it without us. It was His plan from the beginning. Sin couldn't stop it. The devil could not defeat it. He has made us more than conquerors and overcomers in this life for the purpose of working with Him in His plan. We are not laborers for God, we are co-laborers *with* Him.

"We then, as workers together with Him also plead with you not to receive the grace of God in vain" (2 Cor. 6:1).

Even though the scripture refers to the church as an army, we are more than an army. We are more than just workers or slaves. We are not slaves of God, we are sons of God.

"Behold what manner of love the Father has bestowed on us, that we should be called children of God! Therefore the world does not know us, because it did not know Him" (1 John 3:1).

He has brought us into His very own close-knit family. We have been given authority to function as an ambassador of Christ, doing the very works that He did.

"Now then, we are ambassadors for Christ, as though God were pleading through us: we implore you on Christ's behalf, be reconciled to God" (2 Cor. 5:20).

"Most assuredly, I say to you, he who believes in Me, the works that I do he will do also; and greater works than these he will do, because I go to My Father" (John 14:12).

What an amazing place the Father has given us! What a glorious position He has placed us into! We have been raised up with Him and seated with Him in heavenly places, and we are to reign in this life until all His enemies are his footstool. He is counting on us to believe in what He has done and to take our place. He is counting on us to partner with Him and get the job done.

But God, who is rich in mercy, because of His great

love with which He loved us, even when we were dead in trespasses, made us alive together with Christ (by grace you have been saved), and raised us up together, and made us sit together in the heavenly places in Christ Jesus, that in the ages to come He might show the exceeding riches of His grace in His kindness toward us in Christ Jesus.

Ephesians 2:4–7

"For if by the one man's offense death reigned through the one, much more those who receive abundance of grace and of the gift of righteousness will reign in life through the One, Jesus Christ" (Rom. 5:17).

Repent therefore and be converted, that your sins may be blotted out, so that times of refreshing may come from the presence of the Lord, and that He may send Jesus Christ, who was preached to you before, whom heaven must receive until the times of restoration of all things, which God has spoken by the mouth of all His holy prophets since the world began.

Acts 3:19–21

Are you ready to see things change in your life? Are you ready to see God move in the nations? Are you ready to take

your place as a son and partner with God in His great plans?
Are you ready to pray?

PRAY LIKE A RIGHTEOUS MAN

Elijah...A Man in Right Standing

The effective, fervent prayer of a righteous man avails much. Elijah was a man with a nature like ours, and he prayed earnestly that it would not rain; and it did not rain on the land for three years and six months. And he prayed again, and the heaven gave rain, and the earth produced its fruit.

James 5:16b–18

Our prayers should be the kind of prayers that "avail much." They should be the kind of prayers that produce great power. What does it mean to "avail much?" Take a look at what the Amplified Bible says about this verse:

"The earnest (heartfelt, continued) prayer of a righteous man makes tremendous power available [dynamic in its working]" (James 5:16b AMP).

God intended for our prayers to make tremendous power available! Prayer that makes tremendous power available, and prayer that is dynamic in its working, is prayer that meets the qualifications of verse 16. First, we must see and understand that our prayers were intended by God to be powerful and to produce fruit. In verse 16, the two words *effective* and *fervent*, come from one Greek word *energeo*. We get the English word energy from this word *energeo*. It means *to put forth power*. Here, God calls the prayer of a righteous man a prayer that puts forth power. You must begin to see that God's plan for your prayer life is for it to be an activity that brings power on the scene for whatever you are praying about.

Prayer is not to be something that works sometimes, but other times it doesn't. God expects our prayer life to avail much. He expects it to make much power available. Listen to what Jesus said, speaking about our prayer life in John 15:

"If you abide in Me, and My words abide in you, you will ask what you desire, and it shall be done for you. By this My Father is glorified, that you bear much fruit; so you will be My disciples" (John 15:7–8).

The Master is talking about a prayer life that *desires, asks,* and *it comes to pass.* This sounds like the prayer that James is describing. Notice that Jesus says in verse 8 that the Father is glorified "by this." What is the "this" to which Jesus refers? He's referring to desiring, asking, and prayer coming to pass. God is glorified when our prayers come to pass. You see, prayer is to be a certainty. Prayer is supposed to be prayed in confidence, knowing that our Father wants those results more than we do. He is looking for people who know their place in prayer, and who pray with power and authority, believing that their prayer is making tremendous power available.

Once we understand that prayer is intended by God to be effective and to make power available, the second thing we must understand is our prayer must be a prayer that is prayed from a position of righteousness, or right standing with God.

"The effective, fervent prayer of a righteous man avails much" (James 5:16b).

The example of a man praying in right standing with God that James gives us is Elijah. The prophet Elijah had some outstanding results as a result of his prayer life. Here are just a few of those results:

- He increased the oil of the widow of Zarephath is a time of great famine
- He raised the son of the woman of Zarephath from the dead
- He caused rain to fall after years of drought
- He caused fire to consume the water-soaked sacrifice in the showdown in front of the prophets of Baal
- He called fire down upon the soldiers of Ahaziah

How did Elijah get such results? Was it because he was specially anointed or called? Before you answer, look back at what James 5 tells us about him:

"Elijah was a man with a nature like ours, and he prayed earnestly that it would not rain; and it did not rain on the land for three years and six months" (James 5:17).

In other words, there was nothing that made him any different than us. Then how did he get such results? It's simple, and James 5 tells us exactly how…he prayed like a man in right standing with God. It is the prayer prayed as a man in right standing with God that gets powerful results. The effective, fervent prayer of a righteous man avails much. Elijah was a righteous man. He walked in a place of "right-ness" before the Lord. What made Elijah righteous? The same thing that could make any person righteous in the old covenant…obeying the law of God. Obedience to God's laws, and obedience to everything God had said to His people is what gave the people of the old covenant right standing with God. Old covenant righteousness came from obeying God in everything He said, and from carrying out the sacrifices that they had to make in order to atone for their sin. Elijah obeyed God's words and commands, and when he didn't, he made the proper sin sacrifices to cover his disobedience. This gave him right standing, or righteousness.

That was the way old covenant, works-based righteousness worked. If you obeyed all God's commands and performed all His necessary sacrifices and offerings, it gave you a temporary right standing with Him, and you could walk in the blessings of righteousness. The only problem was every time you failed, you had to run back to the sacrifices of God's priesthood, and they had to intercede for you in order to get your sins covered again. Old covenant righteousness was a miserable life of guilt, condemnation, and trying hard to live right in order to be blessed. But how can we pray from a place of righteousness? Do we have to do everything Elijah did? The good news is we are not under the old covenant that was established by the law of Moses; we are under the new covenant that came as a result of Jesus' finished work, and established by the law of faith.

A Righteousness Greater than Elijah

When we hear the word righteousness, most people think right-doing, or right-behaving. That is because most people are more aware of the old covenant than they are the new. The new covenant is entirely different than the old. In the old covenant, under the law of Moses, a person obeyed all the commands and sacrifices and then a temporary righteousness was given to him. If you looked at it like a mathematical equation, it would look like this:

(Obedience by the power and strength of your flesh) = Righteousness

An old covenant person could only stand in righteousness by the power and strength they had. Righteousness was not permanent. It had to be maintained by obedience. It was lost and regained, over and over again. Even though a person went through the proper sacrifices, their heart could never be cleansed. Their heart remained condemned by the continual reminder of all the things they had to do in order to be right.

So much of the church today is still trying to live for God by maintaining a record of good works. They live with a mixture of old and new covenant living, and thereby short-circuit the power of God. Our righteousness today, under the new covenant that Jesus came to bring, is entirely different; and, it is vital for you to know the difference. You cannot live for God with a mixture of the old and new. We are entirely under a new covenant, and our righteousness comes through an entirely different way!

Unlike the old covenant righteousness, our righteousness is not, and cannot be earned or achieved. It is given to us as a gift when we believe in the finished work of the cross of Jesus. His death, burial and resurrection brought to us a perfect righteousness apart from anything for which we can work or perform. Our righteousness is given to us as a gift, and as a result of our faith in Christ.

"For He made Him who knew no sin to be sin for us, that we might become the righteousness of God in Him" (2 Cor. 5:21).

The sinless Christ became sin for us, so that we might be made His righteousness. Not our righteousness, but His. When a person comes to God through, and by, what Jesus did, God gives them perfect righteousness as a gift never earned, only received by faith as a gift!

"For if by the one man's offense death reigned through the one, much more those who receive abundance of grace and of the gift of righteousness will reign in life through the One, Jesus Christ" (Rom. 5:17).

Because of Christ's perfect obedience we have been given a perfect righteousness. A righteousness that did not come through our obedience to God's law, but one that is given to us as a result of Jesus' perfect obedience to the law. My righteousness is of Him! Because of Jesus, we have been made the righteousness of Christ! If you look at New Testament righteousness as a mathematical equation, instead of looking like this:

(Obedience by the power and strength of your flesh) = Righteousness

It would look like this:

Gift of Righteousness = (God's strength empowering our obedience)

We have an even greater righteousness than that of Elijah. His was earned…ours was a gift! He stood in a powerful place of prayer because he worked for his righteousness. We stand in that same powerful place of prayer, where tremendous power is made available, not because of our obedience to the law, but because of our faith in Jesus' finished work. Finished work again defined earlier in the text.

Therefore by the deeds of the law no flesh will be justified in His sight, for by the law is the knowledge of sin. But now the righteousness of God apart from the law is revealed, being witnessed by the Law and the Prophets, even the righteousness of God, through faith in Jesus Christ, to all and on all who believe. For there is no difference

Romans 3:20–22

How righteous are you? You are as righteous as Jesus Himself because you have His righteousness. You have been given Jesus' own righteousness. You stand in that righteousness the moment you believe on Him and accept Him as Lord. We dare not attempt to stand before God in our own righteousness, or else we fail and our prayers are powerless. Our own righteousness is tainted with failed attempts to do what we think it takes to stand before God with confidence. Listen to what the prophet Isaiah said about our own righteousness under the law:

"But we are all like an unclean thing, and all our righteousnesses are like filthy rags;

We all fade as a leaf, and our iniquities, like the wind, have taken us away" (Isa. 64:6).

And now listen to his prophesy of the new covenant righteousness that would come:

No weapon formed against you shall prosper, and every tongue which rises against you in judgment you shall condemn. This is the heritage of the servants of the LORD, And their righteousness is from Me, says the LORD.

Isaiah 54:17

We are now in Christ Jesus, and we stand in His righteousness. We can now stand before God as sin never existed because we stand in Jesus righteousness. No more guilt, no more condemnation, and no more shame. As Hebrews 4:16 tells us, we can now come boldly before the throne of grace because of our gift of righteousness. Now we can pray, not in our own name, but we pray in the name of Jesus Himself! His name is above all other names! Every power, every government, every evil force operating in this world is subject to the name of Jesus, and we stand in His name. We are now found in Him!

"and be found in Him, not having my own righteousness, which is from the law, but that which is through faith in Christ, the righteousness which is from God by faith" (Phil. 3:9).

Is Jesus Lord of your life? Have you accepted His finished work as the payment for your sin? Are you born again? Then you have been made the righteousness of God, and righteousness has been given to you as a gift. You have His righteousness! Say this out loud:

"I am the righteousness of God in Christ Jesus, and I stand before God righteous by Jesus' blood! I stand in righteousness…I live in righteousness…I pray in righteousness, and I get righteous results in prayer!"

A Position that Affects Our Condition

Now that we have a righteous position, this new position will affect our present condition. Never forget that! Position will affect condition. Whatever condition of circumstances you may find yourself in, you now have a position of righteousness that will change it. You may have a condition of sickness in your physical body, but you can change that condition from your spiritual position of righteousness by praying and receiving healing. Now that you are righteous, you deserve to be healed just as much as Jesus deserves it. The nation that you reside in may have conditions of sin, political unrest, war, terrorism and other forms of darkness, but you and other believers have a position of righteousness before God that gives you the right to pray with power and authority that will change the present condition. We can now come before God's throne with righteous boldness and petition for change in nations. God's will is for all nations to be at peace so the gospel of Jesus can be preached and the kingdom of God can be advanced in the world every place. Now that we have a righteous position with the Father, He has made us ambassadors for His kingdom to go reach every nation. No power can stand in our way when we know who we are and what we have.

> *Now then, we are ambassadors for Christ, as though God were pleading through us: we implore you on Christ's behalf, be reconciled to God. For He made Him who knew no sin to be sin for us, that we might*

become the righteousness of God in Him.

2 Corinthians 5:20–21

We have a position given to us by God as a righteous ambassador. We represent His kingdom, just as Jesus did, with power, authority, signs, wonders, and miracles. Our position will change present conditions! Never underestimate the power of your prayers. Stand before God with boldness and pray for your nation, that His kingdom would go forth in power. Stand before evil with confidence that heaven backs you up. We have been given the same position as Jesus had when He was in the earth. He was righteous. We are righteous in Him. He cast out devils, and you can do the same. He performed every miracle that the Father told Him to perform, and you can too. He was a son, you are one too. Now that you have been made righteous, you qualify to do everything that He did, and even more.

Most assuredly, I say to you, he who believes in Me, the works that I do he will do also; and greater works than these he will do, because I go to My Father. And whatever you ask in My name, that I will do, that the Father may be glorified in the Son. If you ask anything in My name, I will do it.

John 14:12–14

What you believe about righteousness grants you access to the miraculous: miraculous praying and miraculous living. As Elijah stood before the nation and declared "It will not rain until I say so," we can stand in a position of righteousness and affect the conditions around us.

Submitting to Righteousness

The life of faith demands that we learn to live by what He has said, not by how we feel. Feelings change but God's word is eternal and never changes. We do not live by how we feel, we live by faith. It is the lifestyle of those declared righteous.

> *For I am not ashamed of the gospel of Christ, for it is the power of God to salvation for everyone who believes, for the Jew first and also for the Greek. For in it the righteousness of God is revealed from faith to faith; as it is written, "The just shall live by faith."*
>
> **Romans 1:16–17**

Everyone wants to have great faith, but what makes faith "great?" The greatest example of faith we have is recorded in Matthew 8. Jesus Himself said it was the greatest faith He had ever seen.

> *Now when Jesus had entered Capernaum, a centurion came to Him, pleading with Him, saying, "Lord,*

my servant is lying at home paralyzed, dreadfully tormented." And Jesus said to him, "I will come and heal him." The centurion answered and said, "Lord, I am not worthy that You should come under my roof. But only speak a word, and my servant will be healed. For I also am a man under authority, having soldiers under me. And I say to this one, 'Go,' and he goes; and to another, 'Come,' and he comes; and to my servant, 'Do this,' and he does it." When Jesus heard it, He marveled, and said to those who followed, "Assuredly, I say to you, I have not found such great faith, not even in Israel!"

Matthew 8:5–10

A Roman centurion was acknowledged by Jesus to having the greatest faith He had ever seen. What gave him this understanding? He understood authority, and how submission to authority worked. Basically he said, "I understand authority, and if you say it, it will happen!" Submission to God and accepting what He says is true is the greatest faith a person can have. Accepting His word as final authority, and holding to it regardless of what you see, hear, or feel is the highest kind of faith.

But what is real submission? Submission is not agreement. To submit means to place yourself under something or someone. Real submission isn't based on how you feel.

Real submission takes place when your will, your opinion, or your feelings are contrary, but you willingly place yourself under the will, opinion, or desire of someone else. If you agree with something that your employer tells you to do, you didn't submit, you agreed. But what if your employer asked you to do something that you didn't feel like doing? Now you have an opportunity to submit.

Submission takes place when you bow the knee to God and say, "I am not who I feel like I am. I am not who I think I am, or what other people say I am. I am who You say I am! If You say I am healed, then that is what I am, even if I don't feel like it. If You say I am righteous by Jesus, then I am righteous even if I don't feel like it!" The apostle Paul understood that we must submit to righteousness because our feelings will be contrary. God is not asking you if you feel righteous or look righteous. He said you *are* righteous. You can choose to stand in your own righteous and fail, or you can stand in the righteousness of Jesus by submitting to what God says about you and succeed.

"For they being ignorant of God's righteousness, and seeking to establish their own righteousness, have not submitted to the righteousness of God" (Rom. 10:3).

Have you submitted to the righteousness that God has given you? Are you declaring boldly in faith that you are the righteousness of God? Do you stand before God in prayer with boldness and confidence as a righteous son, or do you feel like a begging servant? You will access a new power of grace when you submit to righteousness. You will begin to expect God's glory and power to manifest when you begin to operate in faith-righteousness. You will begin to live in a realm of peace like you never thought was possible when you operate in the righteousness of Jesus!

> *Therefore, having been justified by faith, we have peace with God through our Lord Jesus Christ, through whom also we have access by faith into this grace in which we stand, and rejoice in hope of the glory of God.*

Romans 5:1–2

Is your faith in Jesus and His finished work? Then God has declared you righteous. Submit to it and refuse to be moved by how you feel. You now have access to His power by faith and you can pray as a righteous man/woman prays.

Agreeing with the Blood

The blood of Jesus was the very means of exchange that God used to pay for our redemption. Because of Adam's transgression, we were held under the power of sin and under Satan's dominion. We were sinners, and wrath was in our very nature. That's why works righteousness could never work. God had to do it another way, and our nature had to be changed at its core.

And you He made alive, who were dead in trespasses

and sins, in which you once walked according to the course of this world, according to the prince of the power of the air, the spirit who now works in the sons of disobedience, among whom also we all once conducted ourselves in the lusts of our flesh, fulfilling the desires of the flesh and of the mind, and were by nature children of wrath, just as the others. But God, who is rich in mercy, because of His great love with which He loved us, even when we were dead in trespasses, made us alive together with Christ (by grace you have been saved), and raised us up together, and made us sit together in the heavenly places in Christ Jesus

Ephesians 2:1–6

When Jesus shed His blood on the cross, that blood redeemed us out from under sin's power and control. Satan no longer had dominion over us through fear. The blood of Jesus spoke on our behalf. Did you know blood speaks? That's what the scripture tells us! Jesus' blood is speaking and testifying before all of heaven. It is saying, "I have paid the price to the fullest extent! I have bought them and made them righteous! Those that believe in me have the same standing as I have! They are righteous!"

"to Jesus the Mediator of the new covenant, and to the blood of sprinkling that speaks better things than that of Abel" (Heb.12:24).

Pray Like a Righteous Man

When we agree with what the blood is saying about us, we overcome. You have the choice to agree with what fear is saying to you, or what God is saying to you. You have the choice to agree with sickness and pain in your body, or you can agree with the blood. The blood says you are free! The blood says you are healed! The blood says you are qualified for an inheritance from God. Your testimony and what you say is critical. You must not give up from the pressure of circumstances that contradict what the blood of Jesus is saying about you. Agree with the blood! Submit to what He says about you and you will overcome. Revelations tells us that we overcome the devil, the accuser of the brethren, by the blood of the Lamb and by the word of our testimony.

> *Then I heard a loud voice saying in heaven, "Now salvation, and strength, and the kingdom of our God, and the power of His Christ have come, for the accuser of our brethren, who accused them before our God day and night, has been cast down." And they overcame him by the blood of the Lamb and by the word of their testimony, and they did not love their lives to the death.*

> **Revelation 12:10–11**

How Dare She!

Jesus prayed in perfect righteousness. His boldness before the Father caused His disciples to be perplexed and amazed. There was something about the way He prayed and ministered that specifically caught people's attention. The crowds testified, "No man has ever spoke with such authority!" After watching Jesus pray, the disciples came to Him desiring to know what His secret was. His secret was His relationship with Father as a righteous son.

> *Now it came to pass, as He was praying in a certain place, when He ceased, that one of His disciples said to Him, "Lord, teach us to pray, as John also taught his disciples." So He said to them, "When you pray, say: Our Father in heaven, Hallowed be Your name. Your kingdom come. Your will be done On earth as it is in heaven. Give us day by day our daily bread. And forgive us our sins, For we also forgive everyone who is indebted to us. And do not lead us into temptation, But deliver us from the evil one."*

Luke 11:1–4

I've heard this prayer prayed and recited for decades, but I have never heard someone pray it in a way that made me want to ask them, "Wow! Would you teach me to pray like that?" There had to be something about the way Jesus prayed, and not just the words of a prayer. You can hardly read a letter that someone wrote you, and determine the strength, emotion, and fervency that they have. That's what happens when you casually read what we call "The Lord's Prayer" here in Luke 11. If you're not careful, you will miss the spirit of how Jesus prayed...unless you keep reading!

And He said to them, "Which of you shall have a friend, and go to him at midnight and say to him, 'Friend, lend me three loaves; for a friend of mine has come to me on his journey, and I have nothing to set before him'; and he will answer from within and say, 'Do not trouble me; the door is now shut, and my children are with me in bed; I cannot rise and give to you'? I say to you, though he will not rise and give to him because he is his friend, yet because of his persistence he will rise and give him as many as he needs."

Luke 11:5–8

This entire story that Jesus goes into is about a man with a certain quality in his life. It's the same quality that Jesus had before His Father. This quality was a result of His right standing (his assurance of his position and relationship with the Father). This man has the audacity to go to his neighbor's house "at midnight!" Keep in mind, that people in that day went to be much earlier than most of us do. They had nothing to keep them up, like electricity or entertainment, so this man has been asleep for hours.

A late night visitor comes to the man's house, and he notices they are hungry. He marches right out into the night and begins to beat on his neighbor's door and ask for food to feed his hungry visitors. Jesus says that the neighbor's normal response should be to stand behind a closed door and deny him the request due to the lateness of the hour. But that is not what Jesus said would happen. He said the man would rise, open the door and give him what he was requesting "because of his persistence."

The Greek word that is translated "persistence" does not actually mean to keep doing something over and over. It is the Greek word *anaídeia* and it means "to have a quality of shamelessness about one's self." What was it that fascinated the disciples of Jesus and drew them to Him to ask to be taught to pray like He prayed? It was the shamelessness He had before the Father. A boldness and a shamelessness to ask big. A shamelessness to relate to the Father without the sense of guilt, shame, or insignificance. It was His right standing with the Father. It was what fascinated the crowds. It was what drew the sinners. It was what made the Pharisees want to stone Him. Jesus was the first person to walk the earth and reveal what a relationship with God looks like when one is in right standing with God. Jesus was righteous, and because of His love for us and because of His blood… so are you!

PRAYING WHILE SEATED

Jesus Reigns from a Seat

The image that many believers have of prayer is us standing on the earth with so many bad things happening around us, looking up to the heavens, and asking God to come and intervene from heaven. We need to begin to see posture and the position of prayer the way the scripture reveals. Our new righteous position that we have is not us on earth and God in heaven. Our position is not from a posture of kneeling or standing. Our position in heaven is a seat, and the way we reign, pray, worship, and fellowship with the Father is from a seated position. The scripture tells us that now that we are in Christ, we are seated with Him in heavenly places.

> *But God, who is rich in mercy, because of His great love with which He loved us, even when we were dead in trespasses, made us alive together with Christ (by grace you have been saved), and raised us up together, and made us sit together in the heavenly places in Christ Jesus.*

> **Ephesians 2:4–6**

There is a throne in heaven that only one being sits on. It is the throne of God. The Father sits on that throne. The scripture tells us that Jesus sits at the right hand of the Father, and from that seated position He makes intercession for us continually.

"Who is he who condemns? It is Christ who died, and furthermore is also risen, who is even at the right hand of God, who also makes intercession for us" (Rom. 8:34).

"Therefore He is also able to save to the uttermost those who come to God through Him, since He always lives to make intercession for them" (Heb. 7:25).

It is very important to see two things here: First, that Jesus is at the *right hand* of God. Whenever someone sat at the right hand of a king, it symbolized that the king put this person there to signify that this person had all of the king's power at his disposal. The "right hand" was a symbol of power. The king's regents often sat at his right hand. Regents were those who the king had authorized to reign in his place, or in his absence. When a regent made a ruling or a declaration, that ruling had the power of the king behind it. Let's look at some scriptures that refer to Jesus' present position of power and authority:

"Jesus said to him, "It is as you said. Nevertheless, I say to you, hereafter you will see the Son of Man sitting at the right hand of the Power, and coming on the clouds of heaven" (Matt. 26:64).

"Therefore being exalted to the right hand of God, and having received from the Father the promise of the Holy Spirit, He poured out this which you now see and hear" (Acts 2:33).

"But he, being full of the Holy Spirit, gazed into heaven and saw the glory of God, and Jesus standing at the right hand of God" (Acts 7:55).

> *Who being the brightness of His glory and the ex-press image of His person, and upholding all things by the word of His power, when He had by Himself purged our sins, sat down at the right hand of the Majesty on high.*

> **Hebrews 1:3**

Right now, at this moment, Jesus is sitting at the right hand of God in a place of power and authority. The second thing we need to see is that this is a seated position. Kings rule from a throne, or a seated position. A seat is a place of fulfillment. A seat is a place of rest. It is a place of kingdom power and position. When God created the earth in six days, He rested on the seventh, because His work was finished and complete. Creation was perfect in every way and there was nothing else that needed to be done, so God sat down on the seventh day.

When Jesus did everything that needed to be done to se-cure a perfect redemption, He ascended to a place and sat down. There is nothing that needs to be added to creation in order for it to work, and there is nothing that needs to be added to what Jesus did for you to be redeemed completely. It is finished! It is complete! We who have believed are completely forgiven, completely delivered from Satan's power, and completely healed from sickness and disease. Jesus has been given complete authority and power to rule over all the devil's kingdom by completing His earth assignment. His seat is the highest place of power in the heavens and in the earth. He is King of kings and Lord of lords!

And what is the exceeding greatness of His power toward us who believe, according to the working of His mighty power which He worked in Christ when He raised Him from the dead and seated Him at His right hand in the heavenly places, far above all principality and power and might and dominion, and every name that is named, not only in this age but also in that which is to come. And He put all things under His feet, and gave Him to be head over all things to the church, which is His body, the fullness of Him who fills all in all.

Ephesians 1:19–23

Therefore God also has highly exalted Him and given Him the name which is above every name, that at the name of Jesus every knee should bow, of those in heaven, and of those on earth, and of those under the earth, and that every tongue should confess that Jesus Christ is Lord, to the glory of God the Father.

Philippians 2:9–11

A king seated in his seat has nothing to prove. That's why he is sitting down. He has entered into the "rest" of his reign. He carries out his rule of power with his words. He declares something, and it's done. If he were to order that someone in prison be set free, he would not get up off of the seat of his throne and go to the prison and unlock the door. Someone would do that for him. All he does is carry out the rule of his kingdom from his seated position of power.

Seated with Jesus

The most amazing thing about this seat of power at God's right hand is that Jesus doesn't sit there alone. He decided to share it with us. Everything that happened to Jesus in His death— burial, resurrection, ascension, and seating at God's right hand—happened to us too. He chose to unite with us in this work. When He died, you died with Him! When He was buried, you were buried with Him! When He was raised from the dead, you were raised with Him!

Or do you not know that as many of us as were bap-

tized into Christ Jesus were baptized into His death? Therefore we were buried with Him through baptism into death, that just as Christ was raised from the dead by the glory of the Father, even so we also should walk in newness of life. For if we have been united together in the likeness of His death, certainly we also shall be in the likeness of His resurrection, knowing this, that our old man was crucified with Him, that the body of sin might be done away with, that we should no longer be slaves of sin.

Romans 6:3–6

We died with Him, we were buried with Him, and we were raised with Him. We were united together! Death no longer has power over Him, and because we were united together, death no longer has dominion over us. We are more than conquerors of death. Do you understand what it means to be more than a conqueror? Someone who is more than a conqueror receives all the benefits of a conqueror, without having to do the work that the conqueror does.

It's like a professional fighter who trains for years to be the world champion. His dream is to one day stand as champion of the world and receive the multi-million dollar prize from winning the title bout. He daily disciplines himself to eat only the food that brings the maximum nourishment to fuel his body. His daily workouts are rigorous and painful.

He runs miles every day and works out in the gym. Day after day he spars with opponents training for the big fight of his life. He finally gets to the day of the big fight. He has physically and mentally trained and prepared himself for this day.

Round one starts as the bell rings and he begins to exchange brutal blows with the enemy, his opponent. Round two, round three, round four…he is tired and hurting. Round five, six, seven, all the way to the final round, round fifteen. He can barely move, but he keeps fighting. His eyes are swollen shut and he is bleeding from his nose and mouth. The final bell rings and the crowd cheers. The official votes are counted and the decision is in. The referee walks over to him, raises his arm, and declares him to be the new champion of the world! A man dressed in a suit walks over to him and presents him with the prize, the check for $35 million! He has won! He is the new conqueror and champion of the world!

But then something amazing happens…his wife, a petite lady who hasn't trained or sweated one bit for this fight, walks over and takes the check from his hand and kisses him on his bruised cheek. From there she will go and begin to spend that 35 million dollars. He was the conqueror…she was *more* than a conqueror! She gets to enjoy everything he worked for without doing a single thing because she was *united together with* him in marriage! She has a right to the prize without working for it!

You're not a conqueror; you are more than a conqueror! Because we were united together with Jesus in His death, burial and resurrection, we get to enjoy all the benefits of His finished work without having to work for it or earn the prize. He won dominion over sin, sickness, and disease. He won the title of the name which is above every name! He won the highest and most powerful place that can be attained, the seat at the right hand of God. His seat is higher than cancer. Higher than any disease. Higher than any addiction. Higher than any other principality or power, or any name that has been named.

Now that He has won the final battle for the souls of mankind, He has done something so extravagant, so unheard and mind-blowing…He moves over to the side of His chair, pats His hand on His seat, and invites you to sit down with Him! As you sit down with Him in His seat of power and authority, the demons scream "This is unfair!" The Father smiles a smile of joy and satisfaction. Jesus Christ, the son of God, has made room for you to sit down with Him in the highest and most powerful seat in the universe. You are now one with Him, sharing with Him in the inheritance that He has won. How does it feel to be more than a conqueror?

We not only identify with Him in death, burial, and resurrection, but we identify with Him in ascension and in seating.

But God, who is rich in mercy, because of His great love with which He loved us, even when we were dead in trespasses, made us alive together with Christ (by grace you have been saved), and raised us up together, and made us sit together in the heavenly places in Christ Jesus, that in the ages to come He might show

*the exceeding riches of His grace in His kindness to-
ward us in Christ Jesus.*

Ephesians 2:4–7

So many Christians today don't know that when they
were born again, they received a new identity. They have
identified with Jesus in seven ways:

1. They have died with Him. (Rom. 6:3, 5)
2. They were buried with Him. (Rom. 6:4)
3. They were raised with Him. (Rom. 6:4, 5)
4. They ascended to the highest place with Him. (Eph.
    2:6)
5. They were seated with Him. (Eph. 2:6)
6. They received an inheritance with Him. (Rom. 8:17)
7. They now reign with Him. (Rom. 5:17; 2 Tim. 2:12)

We are not on earth praying to a God in heaven. We pray
from our seat. We pray from a position of righteousness, the
very righteousness of Jesus. We carry out the rule of God's
kingdom as a co-regent, seated next to His right hand of
power. This is what it means to reign!

Co-Regents and Kingdom Ambassadors

This word "reign" has enormous meaning. The scriptures tell us that we are to "reign in life" and we are to "reign with Him."

"If we endure, we shall also reign with Him. If we deny Him, He also will deny us" (2 Tim. 2:12).

"For if by the one man's offense death reigned through the one, much more those who receive abundance of grace and of the gift of righteousness will reign in life through the One, Jesus Christ" (Rom. 5:17).

The word "reign" is the Greek word *symbasileuō*. It is the reign carried out by co-regents. It means to possess supreme honor, liberty, or blessedness with the sovereign of the kingdom, as a regent. A regent is a person who governs a kingdom in the minority, absence, or disability of the sovereign. We have been united with Jesus to carry out the reign of the kingdom in the earth. The King has gone away for now but He will return.

Repent therefore and be converted, that your sins may be blotted out, so that times of refreshing may come from the presence of the Lord, and that He may send Jesus Christ, who was preached to you before, whom heaven must receive until the times of restoration of all things, which God has spoken by the mouth of all His holy prophets since the world began.

Acts 3:19–21

The King has gone away and left His co-regents in charge. We are now ambassadors of heaven and the kingdom of our God. He left us with power and authority to reign in His place. He placed us in His seat and told us He would return. We must occupy and advance the kingdom. We must represent the kingdom as Jesus represented it on the earth in Matthew, Mark, Luke, and John. We must do His works and preach and demonstrate the gospel of the kingdom. We must take our place in prayer, the divine communication between us and God. We must make bold declarations in prayer, commanding that His kingdom come and His will be done. We must pray like a righteous man or a righteous woman!

"Now then, we are ambassadors for Christ, as though God were pleading through us: we implore you on Christ's behalf, be reconciled to God" (2 Cor. 5:20).

"For which I am an ambassador in chains; that in it I may speak boldly, as I ought to speak" (Eph. 6:20).

Seated at His Table

We must realize the power that's in our seated position, and we must also realize that our seated position is a position of rest. We reign from a place of resting from our works that we think we need to do to get results. We should realize that Jesus did all the work that needs to be done to secure our victory, and we reign in the authority of His name. His power and His grace works in us and in our circumstances when we are resting and operating in His name.

Our enemy, the devil and his demons, have no power over us because of Jesus and His finished work. When we sit down, we sit with an understanding of this great authority over all the devil's works. The devil himself understands this truth, but he is hoping that you will be ignorant of it. His greatest battle tactic is to keep you ignorant of new covenant truth and deceive you into believing that he has more power and authority than he actually does. If he can keep a person ignorant, he can keep them defeated. Once a Christian begins to see the light of the truth, the devil's plans are exposed, and he is defeated as the Christian begins to walk in this new light.

That doesn't mean that he will stop trying. That doesn't mean that you won't be tempted to get up out of your seat as he hurls his empty accusations and tries to frighten you. Fear is his only weapon. He wants to get you to respond in fear, and in doing so, you get up out of your seat of authority. You must learn to stay seated and enjoy the benefits of your covenant. (Your right standing or your position.)

"You prepare a table before me in the presence of my enemies; you anoint my head with oil; my cup runs over" (Ps. 23:5).

Notice that this verse says that the table at which we are seated and from which we are receiving is not secluded away from the enemy, surrounded by serenity and peace. It says that we are to sit and eat in the presence of our enemies. Picture, if you will, a huge, beautiful table filled with every kind of delicious food with perfect satisfaction and complete nourishment. Picture yourself seated at the table with Jesus, and He keeps picking up the bowls of food and passing them to you, and you are invited to sit and eat the best meal of your life. With every bite of food, healing power rushes through your body. Your very taste buds explode with sensations that cause peace and joy to rush through your soul. All your anxiety subsides and you couldn't worry about anything in your life, even if you tried. What you are receiving partaking of is overwhelming every part of your life!

Then, in the corner of your eye you notice movement. As you turn to see what it is, you begin to recognize what it is. It's an enemy, and he is waving his arms to get your attention. As you turn to hear what he is saying, the anxiety begins to return and the peace you were experiencing as you sat and ate is now overwhelmed with concern. Before you realize it, you are not seated anymore, but standing, giving all your attention to what the enemies around you are saying. Demons of sickness, lack, and hopelessness now have your attention, all the while Jesus is still seated at the table offering you the very food you need to enjoy life abundantly.

You see, God never said that the enemy would be removed from your presence and that you would receive from Him in seclusion and isolation. He said we would eat in the presence of our enemies! We have a choice to turn around and leave the seat of provision, and focus on the work of the enemy, or we can choose to sit down, turn around, and eat from the table of Jesus' provision. Sit down…turn around… and *eat*!

USING LEGALITIES IN PRAYER

God, the Righteous Judge

God is right. He has never been wrong. He is truth and has never been untruthful. He is faithful, and He has never been unfaithful. Everything He has ever done, and every word He has ever said has been right and legal. If He has ever allowed something to happen, it was the "right" thing to do. It doesn't mean that what He allowed was His will, or that it pleased Him. It was just the right thing to do. God operates on the foundation of what is true and what is right. Over and over in the scriptures He is referred to as "the Righteous Judge."

"Far be it from You to do such a thing as this, to slay the righteous with the wicked, so that the righteous should be as the wicked; far be it from You! Shall not the Judge of all the earth do right?" (Gen. 18:25).

"He shall judge the world in righteousness, And He shall administer judgment for the peoples in uprightness" (Ps. 9:8).

"Let the heavens declare His righteousness, For God Himself is Judge. Selah" (Ps. 50:6).

"Oh, let the nations be glad and sing for joy! For You

shall judge the people righteously, and govern the nations on earth. Selah" (Ps. 67:4).

"Finally, there is laid up for me the crown of righteousness, which the Lord, the righteous Judge, will give to me on that Day, and not to me only but also to all who have loved His appearing" (2 Tim. 4:8).

> *For true and righteous are His judgments, because He has judged the great harlot who corrupted the earth with her fornication; and He has avenged on her the blood of His servants shed by her.*
>
> **Revelation 19:2**

When we pray righteously, we must understand that God will not do something that is not right, therefore, we must understand how to pray using legalities. We must intercede with accuracy, based on what is right from His perspective, not based on what we want to see happen. Prayers are heard and answered based on them being prayed according to His will, not according to ours. To use legalities in prayer means to pray accurately, according to the finished work of Jesus.

> *Now this is the confidence that we have in Him, that if we ask anything according to His will, He hears us. And if we know that He hears us, whatever we*

ask, we know that we have the petitions that we have asked of Him.

1 John 5:14–15

God doesn't respond to need. If He did, then we would live in a world where there were no needs. He doesn't respond to desire or even to prayer. He responds to a person who believes in what He has said. He responds to faith in what He has done. He is truth, and everything He has said and done is the truth. When we pray according to the truth, He will move. Crying and begging doesn't move God to act. Faith in what He has said and what He has done moves Him. Faith and only faith moves God.

The finished work of Jesus was all based on legalities. Because of the way God delegated authority in the earth to man, only a man could redeem us. Jesus coming and redeeming us as a man made our redemption legal. His blood being the payment for sin was legal. God making us righteous because of what Jesus did was legal. The devil can't dispute it and accuse God of cheating or doing something wrong. Everything God did in redeeming us, forgiving us, cleansing us, and making us righteous so His Spirit could indwell us was perfectly legal. When we learn the legalities of our redemption, we learn how to petition in prayer and make perfect intercession for people and for nations.

Our Bible is full of legal terms. Terms like judge, adversary, advocate, witness, plea, evidence and more. These are terms that you would hear in a court of law today. In fact, much of what happens in life is exactly how courts are patterned today. You have God, the righteous judge sitting on His throne. You have Satan, who is called the accuser of the brethren in Revelation 12:10, who acts like a prosecuting attorney. You have you and I, who are on the witness stand, defending ourselves against Satan's accusations. Then you have Jesus, our advocate or our lawyer.

Satan, the prosecutor

The devil wants us bound, imprisoned, and even dead. As Revelation 12:10 says, he is always trying to get us to condemn ourselves with his accusations against us. He doesn't do this every once in a while, he does it continually. He never lets up. And he thinks that if he can pile condemnation and accusations against us continually, that eventually we will break and agree with him.

> *Then I heard a loud voice saying in heaven, "Now salvation, and strength, and the kingdom of our God, and the power of His Christ have come, for the accuser of our brethren, who accused them before our God day and night, has been cast down."*
>
> **Revelation 12:10**

Satan was "cast down" and he was defeated when Jesus was raised from the dead. When Jesus was nailed to the cross, Colossians tells us that the accusations that were against us were also nailed to the cross. Under the Old Testament law of Moses, righteousness could only come through doing everything that the law said to do. As long as the law was in place, Satan could accuse us of doing wrong, thereby gaining access to steal, kill, and destroy us by bringing the curse on mankind.

When the curse came, it was legitimate—lawful because it was in accordance with the law—the legal system established by God. If you obeyed, you were protected. If you sinned, destruction would come, and God had to allow it to happen. Why? Because that's the way the system was under the law. Now we are not under the law, but under grace. We don't operate under that old system anymore, but Satan hopes you will never find that out. Even more, he hopes you will never get established in this new covenant where righteousness isn't based on what you do or don't do. It's based on what Jesus did and your faith in that finished work.

"Having wiped out the handwriting of requirements that was against us, which was contrary to us. And He has taken it out of the way, having nailed it to the cross" (Col. 2:14).

"For sin shall not have dominion over you, for you are not under law but under grace" (Rom. 6:14).

The truth is, Satan doesn't have the right to accuse you of anything because now righteousness doesn't come through the law. But if you are ignorant of that truth, he can convince you that you are guilty, and cause you to align your testimony with his accusation, getting you to confess you are guilty and cause you to expect a penalty.

It plays out on the battlefield of your mind like this: The forces of darkness bring thoughts to our minds like "You are guilty! You don't do the things you are supposed to do, and God is now against you. He won't listen to your prayers because you have sinned." He tells us things like "You never do enough to serve God! You never pray enough and you never read your Bible enough! You are an unspiritual person and you deserve to be sick and in lack. Why would God ever want to help someone as unspiritual as you?" The accusation seem to never stop, and as the scriptures tell us, he accuses us day and night. His hope is that you never come to know the truth, because when you know the truth, Jesus said it would make you free!

While all this is going on, where is God? He is where He has always been...on His throne as the righteous judge. He will get involved after your plea. And if you don't know the truth about your redemption in Jesus, you are bound to cave in to the accusations of the enemy and plead guilty based on all you have done. If you do, you will limit what God can do. He will have to allow things to happen, not because He wants to, but because He has to. It's the "right" thing to do because you are agreeing with the enemy and pleading guilty.

Jesus, our advocate

But what if you know the truth? What if every time the enemy tries to pull you into the arena of your works and what you have done, you refuse to leave the arena of His grace and Jesus' finished work? What if he says, "You're guilty, guilty, guilty!" and you say, "Because of Jesus I am righteous, righteous, righteous!" When he screams "You deserve to be condemned!" you scream, "I deserve to be free and forgiven and clean because of what Jesus did for me!" When he says, "You deserve to be sick because you have failed God so many times and now God won't hear you when you pray!" you say, "God always hears me when I pray because I am now the righteousness of God in Jesus!" What if, instead of agreeing with the enemy's accusations, you agree with what the blood is saying about you? What if in the midst of being on trial and accused of sin, you stand up and declare "*I plead the blood of Jesus on my behalf!*"

What happens is the enemy will shut up and sit down because you refuse to agree with him, no matter what he brings against you. Now his turn is over, and it is now time for your advocate Jesus to approach the righteous judge with your defense. He stands and He declares, "You have heard my witness testify that he pleads my blood in his defense, and I would like to present to the court evidence to that plea." He walks over to a place in the holy of holies, and there is a mercy seat with his blood all over it. As everyone listens, they begin to hear the blood of Jesus cry out loud that "Righteousness was purchased for every person, and forgiveness is now freely available for all!"

"*To Jesus the Mediator of the new covenant, and to the blood of sprinkling that speaks better things than that of Abel*" (Heb.12:24).

The blood is speaking right now on our behalf! It cries out we are righteous, forgiven, and free. The choice is ours whether or not we will agree with the blood, or agree with

Satan's accusations. No matter how hard the accusations get, don't let the enemy pull you into the arena of your works. Stay in the blood! Stay in Jesus! Only say what Jesus' finished works say about you!

After Jesus presents "Evidence A" to the court, He then says "Righteous judge (Father), you have heard that even though the enemy has declared that my witness deserves to be sick, my witness has declared and quoted 1 Peter 2:24, that he is healed by my stripes. I would now like to present Evidence B..."

Jesus turns around and lowers His robe, and reveals the scars from the stripes and the beating He took so that we could be healed. The righteous judge then proclaims, "All evidence is accepted, and I now, according to these facts, and according to the bold testimony of this witness, he/she is free, forgiven, healed and delivered from all these accusations!"

You just overcame, but how and why? Not just because of what the blood said, and not just because of Jesus' stripes, but because you used the legalities of redemption to plead your case. You overcame by the blood of the Lamb *and* by the word of your testimony! You see, if what is coming out of your mouth doesn't align with what the blood is saying about you, you won't see victory. It is when we align our words with what the blood and what the stripes of Jesus are saying about us that we prevail, overcome, and get answers to prayers.

Finished work vs. the law: Satan's final defeat

The devil wants people to believe that he is some great,

powerful being who can bring destruction into their lives whenever he wants. If he can keep people from knowing the truth, he can use deception to defeat them. You see, his only tool is deception, and deception only works when people are ignorant to truth.

His strength was only present whenever the law was, and is, in place. As long as righteousness was based on the law, he had a position of accusation that would work. Now that the old covenant system of being righteous by the law is gone, Satan is dethroned. Jesus spoiled him and defeated him by removing the law and making righteousness available on the basis of faith. Satan's final defeat and disarmament was when Jesus nailed the law to the cross and made righteousness available to all who would believe. His final defeat in your life is when you believe that what Jesus did made you righteous apart from the law, only by faith.

And you, being dead in your trespasses and the uncircumcision of your flesh, He has made alive together with Him, having forgiven you all trespasses, having wiped out the handwriting of requirements that was against us, which was contrary to us. And He has taken it out of the way, having nailed it to the cross. Having disarmed principalities and powers, He made a public spectacle of them, triumphing over them in it.

Colossians 2:13–15

Then I heard a loud voice saying in heaven, "Now salvation, and strength, and the kingdom of our God, and the power of His Christ have come, for the accuser of our brethren, who accused them before our God day and night, has been cast down. And they overcame him by the blood of the Lamb and by the word of their testimony, and they did not love their lives to the death."

Revelation 12:10–11

The need for a mediator: real intercession

So what does all this have to do with prayer? Are legalities important when it comes to prayer? Absolutely! The legalities of our redemption are vital when it comes to us receiving what rightfully belongs to us, and when we stand in the gap or intercede for others. What Jesus legally and rightfully did for the world becomes the means by which we can intercede, or mediate, for others and for nations.

A mediator is someone who stands between two parties, endeavoring to bring justice and reconciliation. Jesus was, and is the great mediator, because He stood between God and a fallen world and brought reconciliation on a legal basis.

"For there is one God and one Mediator between God and men, the Man Christ Jesus" (1 Tim. 2:5).

Therefore, if anyone is in Christ, he is a new creation;

old things have passed away; behold, all things have become new. Now all things are of God, who has reconciled us to Himself through Jesus Christ, and has given us the ministry of reconciliation, that is, that God was in Christ reconciling the world to Himself, not imputing their trespasses to them, and has committed to us the word of reconciliation. Now then, we are ambassadors for Christ, as though God were pleading through us: we implore you on Christ's behalf, be reconciled to God. For He made Him who knew no sin to be sin for us, that we might become the righteousness of God in Him.

2 Corinthians 5:17–21

Jesus put one hand on God and one hand on us, and by His death, burial, and resurrection, brought us back together. He was our mediator. He reconciled us to God, then He gave us the ministry of preaching and praying the reconciliation. That means when we pray, we intercede or mediate. We put one hand on the God and one hand on the world and we pray in line with the finished work of Jesus. We use the legalities of the finished work to pray for people and nations. We hold up the blood and we pray that people's eyes would be open to what Christ has accomplished for them. From our seat, we declare with authority that the true gospel would go forth in power to all men. We demand that Satan loose people from blindness and we declare that light to shine in their hearts so that they clearly see the love and grace of God in Jesus!

We have been given the ministry of reconciliation, and with that ministry come the power and the authority to pray and preach in His name. We become mediators and intercessors when we boldly declare truth in His name, both in prayer and in preaching. The devil must bow his knee and obey us when we intercede using the name and the legalities of the finished work of Jesus. Because Jesus is now the head and we take the place of His body in the earth, we can stand before the righteous judge and intercede on people's behalf, praying that their eyes would be opened to all that Jesus has accomplished for them. We can bind the powers of darkness over people and nations, and we can pray that the gospel would go forth in power and in demonstration of the Holy Spirit!

"And I will give you the keys of the kingdom of heaven, and whatever you bind on earth will be bound in heaven, and whatever you loose on earth will be loosed in heaven" (Matt. 16:19).

There is another way we can intercede for others and for the nations, and that is by praying in the Holy Spirit, or in other tongues. The scriptures tell us that when He prays through us in other tongues, He is making intercession for others. The Holy Spirit knows exactly what, when, and how things need to be done. He knows the plans of the Father, and when we yield to Him in prayer, He makes intercession *through us*.

Likewise the Spirit also helps in our weaknesses. For we do not know what we should pray for as we ought, but the Spirit Himself makes intercession for us with groanings which cannot be uttered. Now He who searches the hearts knows what the mind of the Spirit is, because He makes intercession for the saints according to the will of God.

Romans 8:26–27

The groaning spoken of in this verse is speaking of the deep utterances in other tongues that come when we allow Him to give us the utterance to pray. When you do this, you are interceding by allowing Him to intercede through you. When He makes intercession for you, it is made perfectly according to the will of God. The following example is a good way to pray, using legalities, and also using Spirit-led intercession:

"Heavenly Father, I come before your throne of grace because of what Jesus has done for me, and because of what I want to see happen in my nation. I stand before you righteous by the blood of Jesus, and I present myself to you holy and acceptable, all because of what Jesus accomplished for me. He has made me worthy to stand before you as if sin never existed!

I bring before you the nation of _____. Father, Jesus died to reconcile all these people to you. His blood paid the price for every single person in this nation. His blood is crying out to you this day. They have a right to be saved and born again, Father, but the enemy is holding them in darkness, endeavoring to keep them from hearing and seeing the gospel, lest they be saved. From my seated position with you, I take my authority against every way that he is keeping them blind, and I break his power right now. Right now I bind him from what he is trying to do in the nation of _____. I command that the people be loosed from their chains, and I pray that the gospel would go into every corner of this nation freely and unhindered. I ask you Father, Lord of the harvest, to send laborers into this harvest field. I ask that they go forth preaching, teaching and healing and bringing the kingdom of God in power. I ask you for signs, wonders and miracles to be done in the name of Your Son and my Lord Jesus.

Now, Holy Spirit, you know all the details of how this plan of *God needs to be carried out. I now yield to you to intercede for me with groaning and utterances for the nation of _____. Pray through me the Fathers perfect will right now!"*

(Begin praying in other tongues until you feel a release that you are done praying)

Here are the scriptures and the legalities upon which this prayer is based:

"Let us therefore come boldly to the throne of grace, that we may obtain mercy and find grace to help in time of need" (Heb. 4:16).

"For He made Him who knew no sin to be sin for us, that we might become the righteousness of God in Him" (2 Cor. 5:21).

"I beseech you therefore, brethren, by the mercies of God, that you present your bodies a living sacrifice, holy, acceptable to God, which is your reasonable service" (Rom. 12:1).

"That is, that God was in Christ reconciling the world to Himself, not imputing their trespasses to them, and has committed to us the word of reconciliation" (2 Cor. 5:19).

> *But even if our gospel is veiled, it is veiled to those who are perishing, whose minds the god of this age has blinded, who do not believe, lest the light of the gospel of the glory of Christ, who is the image of God, should shine on them.*
>
> **2 Corinthians 4:3–4**

"Therefore pray the Lord of the harvest to send out laborers into His harvest" (Matt. 9:38).

> *Now, Lord, look on their threats, and grant to Your servants that with all boldness they may speak Your word, by stretching out Your hand to heal, and that signs and wonders may be done through the name of Your holy Servant Jesus.*
>
> **Acts 4:29–30**

Likewise the Spirit also helps in our weaknesses. For we do not know what we should pray for as we ought, but the Spirit Himself makes intercession for us with groanings which cannot be uttered. Now He who searches the hearts knows what the mind of the Spirit is, because He makes intercession for the saints according to the will of God.

Romans 8:26–27

PRAYING THE SCRIPTURES

Now this is the confidence that we have in Him, that if we ask anything according to His will, He hears us. And if we know that He hears us, whatever we ask, we know that we have the petitions that we have asked of Him.

1 John 5:14–15

The Word of God reveals the will of God. One way that you can pray according to the will of God is to pray in line with the Word of God. When we pray according to His will, He not only hears us, but according to this verse, He grants our petitions. When you pray according to the Word, it is a guaranteed answered prayer, and we can be confident every time we pray this way.

When a believer in right standing with God declares things in prayer according to the Word, all of hell's power cannot stop that word from coming to pass. Jesus said in Matthew 24:35, "Heaven and earth will pass away, but my words will never pass away." When we put God's words in our heart and in our mouth, it becomes as if God Himself were speaking. The greatest way that you can bring change in your life and in your nation is to stand in the righteousness of Christ and boldly declare His Word in prayer.

In the rest of this chapter, you will find New Testament scriptures that are prayers that are inspired by the Holy Spirit. They are in the Word to give us insight into God's will, and they are there to guide us into a more effective prayer life. Pray each of them over yourself, your family, your friends and your spiritual leaders. After each scripture are prayers and declarations to help guide you in learning to pray the Word. Pray them in faith, and pray them boldly as the righteousness of God! After you pray each scripture, boldly and confidently make the confessions that follow.

Insert your name and/or the names of other people's name in these New Testament prayers:

"Therefore (I) pray the Lord of the harvest to send out laborers into His harvest" (Matt. 9:38). (Add a certain person, neighborhood, city or nation)

After praying this prayer, confess:

> *The Lord is sending Holy Spirit-filled laborers into the harvest field of (insert name, city or nation), and their eyes are being open to the goodness of god and the truth that is in Jesus. Satan, I bind you in the name of Jesus from blinding these people any longer. They are now loosed to hear and respond to the gos-*

pel in Jesus' name!

Therefore I also, after I heard of your faith in the Lord Jesus and your love for all the saints, do not cease to give thanks for you, making mention of you in my prayers: that the God of our Lord Jesus Christ, the Father of glory, may give to you (me) the spirit of wisdom and revelation in the knowledge of Him, the eyes of your (my) understanding being enlightened; that you (I) may know what is the hope of His calling, what are the riches of the glory of His inheritance in the saints, and what is the exceeding greatness of His power toward us (me) who believe, according to the working of His mighty power

Ephesians 1:15–19

After praying this prayer, confess:

I have the spirit of wisdom! The knowledge of the Father comes to me by revelation. My spiritual eyes are flooded with light so I can clearly see His plan for my life. I have understanding of the rich inheritance that is mine in Christ and of the incredible power that works in me when I believe His promises.

For this reason I bow my knees to the Father of our

Lord Jesus Christ, from whom the whole family in heaven and earth is named, that He would grant you (me), according to the riches of His glory, to be strengthened with might through His Spirit in the inner man, that Christ may dwell in your (my) hearts through faith; that you (I), being rooted and grounded in love, may be able to comprehend with all the saints what is the width and length and depth and height, and to know the love of Christ which passes knowledge; that you (I) may be filled with all the fullness of God.

Ephesians 3:14–19

After praying this prayer, confess:

My inner man is strengthened with power by the Holy Spirit. Christ is more and more at home in my heart as I trust Him. My roots go down deep into the love of God and I have great understanding of all the dimensions of His love. The Father is allowing me to experience that love and causing me to be filled with His very fullness.

"And (pray) for me, that utterance may be given to me, that

I may open my mouth boldly to make known the mystery of the gospel" (Eph. 6:19).

After praying this prayer, confess...

By His grace, right now I have utterance and boldness to make known the gospel of Christ.

And this I pray, that your (my) love may abound still more and more in knowledge and all discernment, that you (I) may approve the things that are excellent, that you (I) may be sincere and without offense till the day of Christ, being filled with the fruits of righteousness which are by Jesus Christ, to the glory and praise of God.

Philippians 1:9–11

After praying this prayer, confess:

My love is abounding and increasing more and more as I increase in the knowledge of God and in the ability to rightly discern things. I understand and I am aware of the things that are important and vital, and I am able by the grace of God to prioritize my life, putting God's things first. This causes me to be sincere and without blame until the day of Christ. My life is being filled with evidence that I am the righteousness of God in Christ and bringing great praise and glory to God.

For this reason we also, since the day we heard it, do not cease to pray for you, and to ask that you (I) may be filled with the knowledge of His will in all wisdom and spiritual understanding; that you (I) may have a walk worthy of the Lord, fully pleasing Him, being fruitful in every good work and increasing in the knowledge of God; strengthened with all might, according to His glorious power, for all patience and longsuffering with joy; giving thanks to the Father who has qualified us (me) to be partakers of the inheritance of the saints in the light.

Colossians 1:9–12

After praying this prayer, confess:

By the wisdom and spiritual insight of the Holy Spirit, I am filled with the knowledge of my Father's will. I always walk worthy of my calling and fully please Him in all things. My life is fruitful in everything I do and I am greatly increasing in the knowledge of God. I am greatly strengthened with His power to have patience and to be longsuffering with joy. Thank you, Father, for qualifying me to partake of my inheritance that comes from being a joint heir with Jesus.

"Meanwhile praying also for us, that God would open to us a door for the word, to speak the mystery of Christ, for which I am also in chains" (Col. 4:3).

After praying this prayer, confess:

The Father is opening up doors for the word and giving me the ability to understand and speak out the mystery of Christ.

"Epaphras, who is one of you, a bondservant of Christ, greets you, always laboring fervently for you in prayers, that you may stand perfect and complete in all the will of God" (Col. 4:12).

After praying this prayer, confess:

I, by His power enabling me, will stand perfect and complete in all that my Father desires me to walk in, and all that He desires for me to accomplish.

Therefore I exhort first of all that supplications, prayers, intercessions, and giving of thanks be made for all men, for kings and all who are in authority, that we may lead a quiet and peaceable life in all godliness and reverence. For this is good and acceptable in the sight of God our Savior, who desires all men to be saved and to come to the knowledge of the truth.

1 Timothy 2:1–4

After spending time praying in the understanding and in other tongues for your spiritual leaders and your national leaders, declare this:

My leaders are doing all that is necessary for the gospel to go forth in my city and in my nation with great power. The church of Jesus Christ is growing exceedingly and the kingdom of God is going forth in word and power!

"Now may the God of peace Himself sanctify you (ME) completely; and may your (MY) whole spirit, soul, and body be preserved blameless at the coming of our Lord Jesus Christ" (1 Thess. 5:23).

After praying this prayer, confess:

God is completely setting me apart and His power is preserving my spirit, soul, and body until He comes.

Therefore we also pray always for you that our God would count you (me) worthy of this calling, and fulfill all the good pleasure of His goodness and the work of faith with power, that the name of our Lord Jesus Christ may be glorified in you (me), and you (I) in Him, according to the grace of our God and the Lord Jesus Christ.

2 Thessalonians 1:11–12

After praying this prayer, confess:

I will be counted worthy of the calling of God. I will fulfill all the good pleasure of His goodness. I will fulfill the work of faith with power and His name will be glorified in me, and I in him by His grace.

Finally, brethren, pray for us, that the word of the Lord may run swiftly and be glorified, just as it is with you, and that we may be delivered from unreasonable and wicked men; for not all have faith.

2 Thessalonians 3:1–2

After praying this prayer, confess...

The word of God has free course with all of my spiritual leaders and they are delivered from unreasonable and wicked people.

Now may the God of peace who brought up our Lord Jesus from the dead, that great Shepherd of the sheep, through the blood of the everlasting covenant, make you (me) complete in every good work to do His will, working in you (me) what is well pleasing in His sight, through Jesus Christ, to whom be glory forever and ever. Amen.

Hebrews 13:20–21

After praying this prayer, confess:

My Father is making me complete in every good work to do His will. He is working in me those things that please Him through the finished work of Christ. I give Him glory forever and ever!

PRAYING RIGHTEOUSLY OVER YOURSELF

Building the Foundation First

When it comes to praying effectively over your own life, there are three critical "images" that must be established scripturally in your heart. These images, or the way we see these three things, will become a foundation upon which our entire lives will be built. I learned something about the importance of foundations early in life.

When I was a teenager, I started working for a man who sold satellite dishes to people that were used for watching television. In that day, these dishes were about ten to twelve feet in diameter. They would allow you to receive hundreds of channels on your television. My job was to install the dish at the customer's home after the purchase. The way these dishes work is they are pointed at a band of satellites that rotate with the earth's orbit. These satellites are about 50,000 kilometers from the earth, and they emit a signal towards the earth that, by the time it reaches the earth, is extremely weak. The job of the satellite dish is to collect the signal and reflect it into a small amplifier that in turn sends a stronger signal to the television. Here's the amazing truth that I learned: If the satellite dish I was installing was only a fraction of a degree off, by the time you get 50,000 kilometers in space, you are hundreds of kilometers, perhaps thousands of kilometers away from the satellite for which you are aiming.

This is how vital what we believe about these three areas is. If you are off with the foundations of what you believe, the end results of your life won't be accurate at all. Get the foundation right and everything will work as God intended it. These three areas, or these three images, that are formed in your heart as a result of what you believe, are critical, vital, and decisive!

First, it is *the image of God* or *how you see God*. This image must mainly come from how Jesus revealed the Father in His life and ministry. The people that Jesus taught and ministered to had a completely different view of the Father than He did. He brought a revelation of a Father that was better than we could ever dream, and one that wanted to treat us better than we deserved. What you believe about God creates an image of Him in your heart that will control how you relate to Him. The Jews in that day thought God's main task was rewarding the good and punishing the evil. Jesus came and taught that our image of Him needs to be a Father who wanted to be good to all. A Father who was better than we could ever imagine!

Second is *the image of your enemy, the devil*. If you listen to what many say about the devil, he is some great power who can come into your life and destroy you at will. When you truly understand who he is, and what Jesus has done to defeat him, you will see that there is never any reason to fear him.

Third, and the image that we will focus on in this chapter, is *the way you see yourself.* What you believe about yourself will create an image that will control everything about your life, when it comes to relating to God, and to other people. The way "you see you" will create a foundation upon which to build your life. Get the foundation wrong, and the end result will be millions of kilometers away from what God intended. As you look at praying righteously over yourself, let's first look at who you are now that you are in Christ, and how that is to affect the way you see yourself and the way for you to pray over your life.

Spirit: The Real You

You, the complete package of you, is made up of three parts. To pray righteously over yourself, you have to understand how you are made. You are a spirit, you have a soul, and you live in a body. This simple truth is so very powerful, and it can give you victory in every area of your life.

You are a spirit created in the image of God, and if you are born again in Christ, your spirit (the real you) is perfect. Because of Adam's original sin and fall, every person is born into this world spiritually dead or "spiritually separated from God. Jesus came to "re-connect" you to God by shedding His blood and paying the penalty for your sin. When you receive His payment and make Him Lord of your life, you are born again, and your spirit is what becomes new and perfect. Look at these scriptures:

"Therefore, just as through one man sin entered the world, and death through sin, and thus death spread to all men, because all sinned" (Rom. 5:12).

Therefore, as through one man's offense judgment came to all men, resulting in condemnation, even so through one Man's righteous act the free gift came to all men, resulting in justification of life. For as by one man's disobedience many were made sinners, so also by one Man's obedience many will be made righteous.

Romans 5:18–19

But you have come to Mount Zion and to the city of the living God, the heavenly Jerusalem, to an innumerable company of angels, to the general assembly and church of the firstborn who are registered in heaven, to God the Judge of all, to the spirits of just men made perfect, to Jesus the Mediator of the new covenant, and to the blood of sprinkling that speaks better things than that of Abel.

Hebrews 12:22–24

Because of Jesus, and because you have received what

He has accomplished for us, by making Him Lord of your life, your spirit has been made perfect. Perfectly whole, perfectly blessed, and perfectly righteous! There is absolutely nothing that needs to change about you, that is, about the real you, your spirit. Change means to become something that you are not. If your spirit needed something, or if it was insufficient in any way, it would need to change. It would need to become what it was lacking, but it lacks nothing. You cannot improve something that's perfect. Your spirit is able to stand before God as if sin never existed. You are not a sinner; you have been made a saint! There is no such thing as a person who is a sinner saved by grace. If you have been saved by His grace then you are not a sinner anymore. You are the righteousness of God in Christ. Now you must see yourself that way. If you don't see yourself that way, you will pray amiss. You will pray over yourself in ways that are unscriptural, that are not according to God's will, the Bible.

"and you are complete in Him, who is the head of all principality and power" (Col. 2:10).

So how are you supposed to pray over your spirit? You're not! All you have to do is agree with what God has done in you and what He says about you. Your spirit needs nothing except the agreement of your heart in faith. There is nothing your spirit needs. You are spiritually in a perfect relationship with the Father because of what Jesus has done. Your spirit is whole, new, righteous, blessed, free, forgiven, and redeemed. Nothing about you (your spirit) needs to change, but there is a part of your being that needs to be transformed…your soul.

Your Soul: Meditation that Brings Transformation

You are a spirit and you have a soul. Your soul is made up of your mind (thoughts), your will, and your emotions (feelings). If you don't know this, you will believe that what you feel is what is true about you. You are not a soul, you are a spirit who possesses a soul. There is absolutely nothing that needs to change about you...that is about the real you, your spirit, but there is much that needs to be transformed about your soul.

As spirit beings, you cannot let your soul dictate who you are or what direction your life is headed. Just because you feel a certain way doesn't mean it's true. You must allow your spirit to dictate truth in your life, and you must transform your soul with the truth of God's word. You can pray righteously over yourself by understanding the work of transformation that must take place in your soul, or your mind, will, and emotions.

"And do not be conformed to this world, but be transformed by the renewing of your mind, that you may prove what is that good and acceptable and perfect will of God" (Rom. 12:2).

Meditation is a form of prayer. Meditate means to ponder something over and over. It also means to mutter, or to speak over and over. To take a truth from God's word, and ponder it, and speak it over yourself, is to meditate righteously, or to pray righteously. When you do this, it brings transformation to the soul. It aligns your sometimes rebellious soul to the truth of who you are in your spirit. It brings the soul into subjection to your spirit. You cannot allow your souls to dominate us. If you do, you will be driven by your thought life and your feelings. As believers, we don't live by how we feel…we live by faith!

"For we walk by faith, not by sight" (2 Cor. 5:7).

To take the truth of who you are in Christ and to meditate on it is a form of praying righteously over yourself. You should spend a good deal of time meditating and praying. Many people only see prayer as going to God and asking Him for things. Prayer is much more than asking and receiving. Meditation is prayer, too, and you should do as much or more meditation than you do asking and receiving. The following is an example of righteously praying and meditating over yourself. Say this over and over, spending time thinking about it, visualizing it and worshipping God because of it. Begin to sense the transformation that it brings in your soul.

"Father, I thank You that you have made me righteous in Jesus! I am now the righteousness of God in Christ. Sin has no dominion over me. I am a master over sin because of this righteousness. I now stand in Your presence as if sin has never been. I am free and forgiven. I am complete in You, and between us there is nothing missing or broken. You see me as a son, belonging to You and born of You. There is no condemnation coming from You, ever. My past is gone and I am brand new in You. I now reign in life because of the abundance of grace You have given me, and because of the gift of righteousness!"

You can pray righteously over yourself like this in any area. Spend time meditating on your righteousness, your sonship, your freedom, and in areas that reveal who you are in Christ. It doesn't change anything about the spirit, but it transforms everything about your soul. Change is an effort to become something that you are not…Transformation is an effortless becoming of who you already are. This understanding creates a big difference in the way you see things. You are not someone who is deficient who needs to change. You are complete and you need the soul transformation of becoming who you already are in Christ Jesus.

The word "transform" in Romans 12:2 is the Greek word *metamorphu*. In English, we get our word "metamorphosis" from this word. It is seen in the process that takes place when a caterpillar becomes a butterfly. If you were to see a caterpillar crawling on the ground, you would think that its destiny is to always be that way. You would think, "Poor little worm, all he can do is slowly crawl on his belly and see things from a lowly perspective!" Little would you know that one day he will see from an even higher perspective than you, because one day he will soar and fly above the trees.

How could this worm ever become a butterfly? By a process called "metamorphosis." You see, this little worm keeps crawling, until one day he begins to sense within him a "cry to fly." He begins to become in touch with his destiny. He begins to sense that his future will be greater than his past and present circumstances. This cry to fly becomes so strong in him that it leads him to ascend into a tree, and there he is led to wrap himself in a cocoon. There, shut away from all outside influences, he enters into a rest where something supernatural begins to take place. Scientists tell us that the caterpillar actually liquifies into a slimy, fluid-like substance as the metamorphosis takes place. When it is complete the beautiful butterfly breaks out of the cocoon and begins to fly, never to crawl again.

The caterpillar did not change. The caterpillar was transformed. You may ask, "What is the difference?" Change is to become something that you are not. Transformation is to become something that you already are. The caterpillar was always destined to become the butterfly, and the butterfly DNA was always inside the caterpillar. That is exactly the way it is with you and me! When you are born again, your spirit is complete, and you possess the DNA of God Himself inside you. What is in you must be put on you. When you renew your mind with the truth of who you are and what God has made you to be, a metamorphosis takes place. The key to getting what is in you to manifesting around you is to renew your mind.

"And be renewed in the spirit of your mind, and that you put on the new man which was created according to God, in true righteousness and holiness" (Eph. 4:23–24).

The word "spirit" here in verse 23 refers to the "general area" of your mind. When you renew your mind, or our soul, you put on what is already in you . A transformation takes place. In you is "a cry to fly!" When you understand this, it gives you a hope that you will not always be in your present circumstances. You, the real you, has been created by God in true righteousness and holiness. The limits that you feel are not because you need something because you are incomplete or insufficient. The limits that you feel come from a soul that is in need of transformation. Your soul is limiting the expression of the new nature that is in your spirit.

So how do we pray righteously over our soul? You do so through the prayer of *meditation*. Meditation is a form, or a kind of prayer. It is vital that you understand that prayer is not just asking God for things. Prayer is not just a small, dedicated time of your day that you set aside for God. There are many kinds of prayer and many ways that those different kinds of prayer are voiced.

"Praying always with all prayer and supplication in the Spirit, being watchful to this end with all perseverance and supplication for all the saints" (Eph. 6:18).

Here is this same verse in the Amplified version of the Bible:

> *Pray at all times (on every occasion, in every season) in the Spirit, with all [manner of] prayer and entreaty. To that end keep alert and watch with strong purpose and perseverance, interceding in behalf of all the saints (God's consecrated people).*
>
> **Ephesians 6:18 (AMPC)**

Here is the same verse in the Phillips translation:

"Pray at all times with every kind of spiritual prayer, keeping alert and persistent as you pray for all Christ's men and women" (Eph. 6:18 PHILLIPS).

You see from this scripture that there are many kinds of prayer. Without going into details, here are a few kinds or types of New Testament prayer:

- The prayer of faith, or asking and receiving
- The prayer of petition
- The prayer of intercession
- The prayer of supplication
- The prayer of worship
- The prayer of unity
- The prayer of speaking in tongues
- The prayer of meditation
- The prayer of declaration
- The prayer of consecration

You could scripturally say, that any means of spiritual communing with the Father, the Son, or the Holy Spirit can be classified as a kind, or type, of prayer.

The kind of prayer that has a great effect on your soul is the prayer of meditation. Meditation means to ponder, to reflect, to mutter, to imagine, and to speak out. Meditation is when you take the truth of God's Word and ponder it, reflect on it, mutter it, speak it, and imagine ourselves walking in the reality of it. When we correctly meditate on truth, the Holy Spirit, who lives in us to help bring about transformation, supernaturally causes a metamorphosis to take place. Your unrenewed soul begins to be renewed and come into an alignment with the born-again spirit, the real you.

Here is how to do this: Let's take 2 Corinthians 5:17 and pray the prayer of meditation. Here's what it says:

"Therefore, if anyone is in Christ, he is a new creation; old things have passed away; behold, all things have become new" (2 Cor. 5:17).

Now, take some time to ponder and think about what this is saying. Without saying it out loud, let these thoughts fill your mind:

"I am now in Christ, and everything about me is now new!"

"Everything old, that is, everything in my past is now gone. It doesn't even exist anymore!"

"A new freedom is now mine! A new way of living is now mine. I now live in the 'God-kind' of life!"

"The nature of sin that I once possessed is now gone! I am now the righteousness of Jesus Christ! His righteousness is now my righteousness!"

Go back over these thoughts and begin to mutter them quietly over and over. Let them move from thoughts to quiet words.

Now, go back over them again, this time pausing in between each statement and use your imagination to picture what your life will look like as the truths begin to be lived out.

For example:

"The nature of sin that I once possessed is now gone! I am now the righteousness of Jesus Christ! His righteousness is now my righteousness!"

(Imagine and get an inner picture of this being lived out,

and picture things that you struggled with falling off of the new you like broken chains falling to the ground.)

To finish this meditation prayer, now declare the same phrases boldly and loudly over your life.

Friend, this is meditation, and this is prayer. It is the way to renew your mind and bring it into alignment with the real you, the spirit, so that your life is not held back anymore by an unrenewed soul that hasn't been transformed. Can you sense the transformation taking place as you meditated on 2 Corinthians 5:17? That transformation is taking place in your soul. This is how we pray righteously over our soul!

Our Body: Commanding it to Change!

You need to learn to pray righteously over one more thing. It's the part of you that keeps the real you, the spirit, here on this earth. When it is destroyed, or when it wears out, the real you, the spirit will leave it and go to be present with the Father…it is your body.

So we are always confident, knowing that while we are at home in the body we are absent from the Lord. For we walk by faith, not by sight. We are confident, yes, well pleased rather to be absent from the body and to be present with the Lord.

2 Corinthians 5:6–8

Just like we discussed in the first chapter, God needed a body to accomplish our redemption. Thus, Jesus came to earth in the form of man. It was His body that gave Him the right to function on the earth, and it is your body that keeps you here. In order for you to fulfill what God has called you to do, you need a healthy body.

This is why Jesus bore our sicknesses and diseases in His own body on the cross, so we could live healthy on the earth. He provided healing for our body just like He provided forgiveness of sin. Healing is a right and a privilege of every born-again child of God. It is something that has already been provided, therefore, it is something that we can appropriate by the prayer of faith and the prayer of declaration.

While living on this earth, if we ever find ourselves in a time where sickness or disease tries to infiltrate our body, we can receive healing by faith, and with authority command our bodies to change and line up with God's word. It is not up to God to heal you, as if healing hasn't been provided, yet many today inaccurately pray that way. They pray prayers like "Father, please heal my body" or "Lord, please heal so-and-so." You may ask "Why is this inaccurate when it comes to prayer?" The reason is because God will not redo something that He has already done.

It would be like you preparing a meal for one of your children, and them coming to the table that is spread with food and looking at you and asking you, "Could you please give me something to eat?" How would you react if that happened? You would point to the food that you already prepared and say, "Eat, child, it has already been prepared!"

What Jesus accomplished and provided for us over 2,000 years ago is like a vast meal that the Father has spread before us. Enjoying the benefit is not a matter of the Father feeding it to us like you would an infant child, but as we grow and renew our minds we must learn to appropriate what He has so lovingly and graciously provided. He would say to you, "Eat, my child, healing has been provided!"

> *Surely He has borne our griefs and carried our sorrows; Yet we esteemed Him stricken, smitten by God, and afflicted. But He was wounded for our transgressions, He was bruised for our iniquities; The chastisement for our peace was upon Him, and by His stripes we are healed.*
>
> **Isaiah 53:4–5**

"Who Himself bore our sins in His own body on the tree, that we, having died to sins, might live for righteousness—by whose stripes you were healed" (1 Peter 2:24).

Healing belongs to us and it is our inheritance because of Jesus. God decided in Jesus for all who would receive to be saved, healed, and free in spirit, soul and body. He doesn't have to decide anymore. It is available to whosoever will believe it and receive it! Knowing this, how should we pray righteously over our bodies? We pray the prayer of faith and believe that we receive it, then we use our authority as a righteous son to command things to change.

> *So Jesus answered and said to them, "Have faith in God. For assuredly, I say to you, whoever says to this mountain, 'Be removed and be cast into the sea,' and does not doubt in his heart, but believes that those things he says will be done, he will have whatever he says. Therefore I say to you, whatever things you ask when you pray, believe that you receive them, and you will have them."*

Mark 11:22–24

Verse 24 says when we pray, we are to believe that we receive the very thing that we are praying for. We can do this when it comes to something that God has already said belongs to us. Healing belongs to us because of Jesus, so when we stand before God, communing with Him, He expects us to reach out with our heart and take hold and receive what we are wanting.

The real you, the spirit, fits inside your body like a hand would fit inside of a glove. Your body is the "glove" of your spirit. Just like your body has certain members, your spirit does too. In fact, every member of your body is a reflection of your spirit. Just as you have a tongue that has taste buds causing you to physically taste things, your spirit can taste things as well.

"Oh, taste and see that the Lord is good; Blessed is the man who trusts in Him!" (Ps. 34:8).

When you trust God, or when you walk by faith, you can "taste" spiritual things. Also, just as your body has ears that hear physical sounds, your spirit can hear spiritual sounds when you live by faith and trust God.

"He who has an ear, let him hear what the Spirit says to the churches" (Rev. 2:7).

As with eyes and ears to see and hear, your body has arms and hands that cause it to be able to grab and seize and take hold of things in this physical world. Your spirit also has members that you use to grab and take hold of things spiritually. You can "take hold" or receive something with your heart, just like you can with your physical body. When Mark 11:24 says that we are to "believe that we receive" things when we pray, the word "receive" is the Greek word *lambano*. *Lambano* means to take hold, to lay hold, to seize or to take to one's self.

When it comes to praying righteously over our bodies, we can go before the throne of God and "take" healing. Without asking, without bargaining, without pleading. Why? Because it is our inheritance. Jesus paid a great price so you and I could have it. I can walk right up to the table of provision, and boldly declare with faith and thanksgiving:

"Father, thank You for healing me over 2000 years ago and making healing available for me today! Right now, with the arms of my heart, I reach out and take healing to myself! I receive it, and right now, I have it. It's mine! My body is

healed by the stripes of Jesus!"

Once you receive it according to Mark 11:24, now begin to pray the prayer of authority and declaration according to verse 23:

> *For assuredly, I say to you, whoever says to this mountain, 'Be removed and be cast into the sea,' and does not doubt in his heart, but believes that those things he says will be done, he will have whatever he says.*

Mark 11:23

Begin to declare boldly over your body:

"My body is healed by the stripes of Jesus! I command all sickness, disease, pain and weakness to leave my body now in the name of Jesus!"

As you pray this righteous prayer of declaration, believe that what you are saying is coming to pass. Believe that your words have power as a righteous son of God. Believe, and refuse to doubt that everything you said will come to pass and God's healing power will work mightily in your body. It's a guarantee! These are the very words of Jesus Himself here in Mark 11. If we take Him at His word and act in faith, it must come to pass. Don't let pain move you away from the promise. Don't let a doctor's report move you off of your faith! Jesus said if you would believe that you receive it, *you would have it*! Take Him at His word and walk by faith, not by sight.

PRAYING RIGHTEOUSLY FOR OTHER PEOPLE

How to Pray for Believers

From God's perspective, there are three groups of people on the earth. These three groups can actually be narrowed down into two groups of people. These three groups are:

- Jews, or the nation of Israel
- Gentiles, or people outside of the nation of Israel

And because of Jesus and what He has done, God now sees a third group,

- The Church, or Jews and Gentiles that have received Christ as Messiah and Lord

"Give no offense, either to the Jews or to the Greeks (Gentiles) or to the church of God" (1 Cor. 10:32).

In order to be saved, both Jews and Gentiles must be born again and receive Jesus as Lord. Jesus is *the only* way to be saved. He is the way, the truth and the life!

"Jesus said to him, "I am the way, the truth, and the life. No one comes to the Father except through Me" (John 14:6).

When Jesus said "no one" He meant "no one!" So because of this statement by Jesus Himself, God actually only sees two groups of people: saved people who have received Jesus and unsaved people who have not received Jesus. Realizing that God only sees two groups of people, we must learn how to righteously and effectively pray for these two groups. We must understand how to pray for believers and how to pray for unbelievers. Why? One group is in a covenant with Almighty God through Jesus. The other group stands outside the covenant and are "aliens and outsiders" according to Ephesians and Colossians. Because people are different, they must be prayed for differently.

This I say, therefore, and testify in the Lord, that you should no longer walk as the rest of the Gentiles walk, in the futility of their mind, having their understanding darkened, being alienated from the life of God, because of the ignorance that is in them, because of the blindness of their heart.

Ephesians 4:17–18

Praying Righteously for People

"And you, who once were alienated and enemies in your mind by wicked works, yet now He has reconciled" (Col. 1:21).

Believers are redeemed by the blood of Jesus because they have confessed Jesus as the Lord of their life. They have been freed from sin and forgiven from all sin. They have a binding agreement with God that the scripture refers to as a covenant. A covenant is the strongest of all agreements that exists. The punishment for breaking covenants was usually death. When two people, two nations, or two families entered into a covenant together, it was to last forever.

God is the originator of covenant. He initiated the covenant between Himself and Abraham that we refer to as the Abrahamic covenant. When He gave the law to Moses, He made a covenant with Israel. These covenants were between God and men, and had fault in them because men could break them. God always kept His side of the covenant, but man always failed. That's why it says in Romans that the law was weak. It wasn't weak from God's side, only from man's side.

For what the law could not do in that it was weak through the flesh, God did by sending His own Son in the likeness of sinful flesh, on account of sin: He condemned sin in the flesh, that the righteous requirement of the law might be fulfilled in us who do not walk according to the flesh but according to the Spirit.

Romans 8:3–4

Our new covenant is different from any other covenant, because it was made between God the Father and Jesus. We get in on it because Jesus represented us and stood in the covenant for us. It cannot be broken! It will never end! When we fall, sin, or do things that would normally break a covenant, the covenant still stands because the two parties that made the covenant can never lie, sin, or break covenant. God made an eternal covenant with Jesus, the Son of Man; therefore, all men who receive Jesus get in on it. We can now receive all the benefits of the covenant in Jesus' name, and on His behalf. Our worthiness to walk in covenant is never determined by our actions, but by the actions of one man, the man Christ Jesus! Hallelujah!

Now, we believers join in the covenant with Jesus. We are heirs to the inheritance of all that God has and all that He is. We are in Christ! We receive because of Jesus. We are healed because of Jesus. We can prosper and be blessed because of Jesus' obedience. We have the same righteous standing as Jesus because we are in Him. All of these blessings are not something that God will do for us when we perform up to His standards. They are ours legally by inheritance, and it was all God's idea. He did it because of His great love for us. Believers have rights and believers have privileges because of covenant. The problem is so many believers don't know it. They perish because of a lack of knowledge.

"My people are destroyed for lack of knowledge" (Hosea 4:6).

The most important thing for any person to have is light. Satan's greatest strategy is to keep people in the dark so they can never see the truth. We move from a place of ignorance to a place of understanding when light shines on the truth. As long as people stay in the dark, they continually will stay in defeat. Once light comes, the enemy's strategies are destroyed. He has no power to destroy, only power to deceive. Jesus destroyed his work and took away the keys of death, hell, and the grave. Satan's only strategy is deception, but light destroys his strategy.

> *But even if our gospel is veiled, it is veiled to those who are perishing, whose minds the god of this age has blinded, who do not believe, lest the light of the gospel of the glory of Christ, who is the image of God, should shine on them.*

2 Corinthians 4:3–4

When unbelievers remain in darkness, they remain unsaved. When believers walk in darkness, they are saved, but they remain defeated. This is why we must pray for them, but praying righteously and accurately is the only way we can get results. Believers have a covenant, but might be ignorant of it, and therefore walk as if they have no covenant. So how can we pray for believers? By praying for them like the apostle Paul prayed for them: by asking God to flood their hearts with light.

Therefore I also, after I heard of your faith in the Lord Jesus and your love for all the saints, do not cease to give thanks for you, making mention of you in my prayers: that the God of our Lord Jesus Christ, the Father of glory, may give to you the spirit of wisdom and revelation in the knowledge of Him, the eyes of your understanding being enlightened; that you may know what is the hope of His calling, what are the riches of the glory of His inheritance in the saints, and what is the exceeding greatness of His power toward us who believe, according to the working of His mighty power which He worked in Christ when He raised Him from the dead and seated Him at His right hand in the heavenly places, far above all principality and power and might and dominion, and every name that is named, not only in this age but also in that which is to come.

Ephesians 1:15–21

Paul, being inspired and led by the Holy Spirit, utters a powerful prayer for the believers in the Ephesian church. He doesn't ask God to do anything that He has already done in the finished work of Jesus. He simply prays that their hearts would be flooded with light, and by that light they would be able to see what has already been done for them in Christ.

Praying Righteously for People

The Holy Spirit, through Paul, is teaching us how to pray for believers. We are to pray that they would be able to see what they need to see and that they would not be blinded from the truth any longer.

Believers need to see and understand God's will for their lives. We cannot have faith until we understand what God's will is. Many believers are perishing today because they don't know God's will. They don't know how to claim their inheritance by faith. When the Holy Spirit shines light on the word of God, we now see the will of God and we can have faith. Here we see that we, as believers, we can pray for other believers for their eyes to be opened. This way they can see and understand those things about which they are ignorant of. Paul prays again for the church in Colossae in the same way.

For this reason we also, since the day we heard it, do not cease to pray for you, and to ask that you may be filled with the knowledge of His will in all wisdom and spiritual understanding; that you may walk worthy of the Lord, fully pleasing Him, being fruitful in every good work and increasing in the knowledge of God; strengthened with all might, according to His glorious power, for all patience and longsuffering with joy

Colossians 1:9–11

Here Paul prays for believers to be filled with the knowledge of God's will. He doesn't pray that God would heal them, He prays that they would be filled with the knowledge that it is God's will for them to be healed because they were healed in Jesus' finished work. He doesn't ask God to bless them because that's something that God has already done in Christ. He is praying for them to be filled with the knowledge that God has already blessed them, and they can now have faith to walk in the blessings of God.

"Blessed be the God and Father of our Lord Jesus Christ, who has blessed us with every spiritual blessing in the heavenly places in Christ" (Eph. 1:3).

When we pray for believers, we pray for them to be filled with the knowledge of their covenant; to be filled with the understanding of all their rights and privileges in Christ. To ask God to do something for them that He has already done is to ask amiss. That is praying unscriptural prayers. If we want New Testament results, we're going to have to pray according to the New Testament.

How to Pray for Unbelievers

Unbelievers are people that the scriptures refer to as being "lost." They are lost because Jesus is not the Lord of their lives. Romans 10:9–10 describe to us how a person who is lost can be saved from the present darkness that they live in.

That if you confess with your mouth the Lord Jesus

and believe in your heart that God has raised Him
from the dead, you will be saved. For with the heart
one believes unto righteousness, and with the mouth
confession is made unto salvation.

Romans 10:9–10

When a lost person believes in the gospel of Jesus Christ
and His finished work and confesses Jesus as his Lord, he or
she is born again from death and darkness to life and light.
They are put into God's kingdom and they become one of
God's own children.

"He has delivered us from the power of darkness and
conveyed us into the kingdom of the Son of His love, 14 in
whom we have redemption through His blood, the forgive-
ness of sins" (Col. 1:13–14).

There are certain things that have to happen in order for
people to be saved. The process, or the way these things
have to happen, can teach us how to pray for people who are
not saved, people we refer to as unbelievers. We see from
the scriptures above that in order for them to be saved, they
must to call on Jesus, but how can they if they have never
heard about Him and the work that He accomplished so we
could be forgiven? Listen to how Romans explains the process, and thereby shows us how we can effectively pray for
unbelievers.

For "whoever calls on the name of the Lord shall be
saved." How then shall they call on Him in whom

they have not believed? And how shall they believe in Him of whom they have not heard? And how shall they hear without a preacher? And how shall they preach unless they are sent? As it is written: "How beautiful are the feet of those who preach the gospel of peace, who bring glad tidings of good things!"

Romans 10:13–15

Here are the things that must happen in order for an unbeliever to be saved according to this passage:

First, verse 15 says there must be a sending of preachers. When we pray for lost souls, we must first pray that preachers be sent into the unbelievers lives. God will send people across their paths to bring the message of Jesus to them when we ask. Jesus instructed His disciples to pray this very same way.

Then Jesus went about all the cities and villages, teaching in their synagogues, preaching the gospel of the kingdom, and healing every sickness and every disease among the people. But when He saw the multitudes, He was moved with compassion for them, because they were weary and scattered, like sheep having no shepherd. Then He said to His disciples, "The harvest truly is plentiful, but the laborers are few. Therefore pray the Lord of the harvest to send out laborers into His harvest."

Matthew 9:35–38

When we pray for unbelievers, we must first ask the Father to send laborers, or preachers, to them. We should pray, *"Father, you see these people that don't know You, and who are lost without You. We ask you, in the name of Jesus, to send preachers of the gospel into these people's lives. Send preachers of the finished work of Jesus! Send preachers and equip them with miracles and signs and wonders. Let the gospel not only be preached in word only, but let it be demonstrated in the power of the Holy Spirit!" Send me—create the fruit of my lips so that I may have the word to speak to them.*

Second, we must pray that the people hear the message. The devil doesn't want people to hear because he knows that when they do, they will call on Jesus and be saved. He is the master of deception and distraction. His only tool is to try and blind people from seeing God's love and His goodness, and from seeing the salvation that God is offering them through Jesus.

But even if our gospel is veiled, it is veiled to those who are perishing, whose minds the god of this age has blinded, who do not believe, lest the light of the gospel of the glory of Christ, who is the image of God, should shine on them.

2 Corinthians 4:3–4

The devil, who is the god of this age, has blinded these lost people, and their only hope is that someone will come with light and help them see. When we pray for unbelievers, we must use our God-inherited authority that is in the name of Jesus to break and stop the devil's blindness that is over the hearts of unbelievers. We should pray, *"Father, in the name of Jesus I break Satan's power of blindness, deception and distraction over these people! I declare that when the gospel is preached to them, they will see and hear the goodness of God clearly, with no distraction, and with perfect understanding!"*

Third, the unbeliever must respond by calling on Jesus. To openly confess Jesus as Lord takes courage and boldness. We should pray that people would have a bold faith in Christ. We should pray that the power of timidity and fear be broken in their life, and that they would have a freedom to confess Jesus openly and publicly without shame. Our faith in Christ is not something that we receive timidly and hide for the rest of our lives. We live for Him openly and boldly, and we are not afraid to even die for Him. God grants people this boldness when we ask Him. We should pray, *"Father, grant that these people have a fearless boldness to accept Jesus as Lord, and that they not be ashamed of the testimony of Jesus. Right now, we take authority over the fear that would cause them to draw back from Christ! May they be unashamed of Your love and Your power!"*

"For whoever is ashamed of Me and My words in this adulterous and sinful generation, of him the Son of Man also

will be ashamed when He comes in the glory of His Father with the holy angels" (Mark 8:38).

PRAYING RIGHTEOUSLY FOR NATIONS

Praying for those in Authority

Can a believer pray and affect nations? Can believers in a nation that does not promote or even accept Christianity pray and bring change to the nation? The answer is absolutely and emphatically "*Yes!*" Why would the Lord instruct us in His word to pray for people and for nations if He did not intend to bring those prayers to pass by answering them in power and authority? If He asks us to pray, then He intends to move when we obey Him.

There is no such thing as a nation where God will not move when we pray. There is no nation too dark and ungodly to stand against God's power. No matter what the leaders of that nation have done or decreed, God will have the final word. His heart is to see a harvest of souls come from every nation. Jesus died for them to be saved and He raised up a church, filled them with His power, and sent them to the nations to be a witness. He sent us the church to pray and intercede, and He sent us to preach the gospel to all who are lost. He will do His part, and we must do our part.

Therefore be patient, brethren, until the coming of the Lord. See how the farmer waits for the precious fruit of the earth, waiting patiently for it until it receives the early and latter rain. You also be patient. Establish your hearts, for the coming of the Lord is at hand.

James 5:7–8

Like a patient farmer waiting on the ripening of the harvest, God is waiting on the precious fruit of the earth. He wants to send rain on those fields. Rain is a type and shadow of the power and the presence of the Holy Spirit. The work of the Holy Spirit through the church is what will ripen the harvest and bring it into the harvest barns. God will use all of His great power and resources to bring in His harvest. It is precious to Him. Every nation is precious!

A harvest is not complicated. It's a simple process that is involved in reaping a great harvest. First, there is the breaking up of the ground, and the planting of the seed. Then there is rain. Then there is patience. Then there is more rain... then there is harvest! What does this process teach us about praying for nations?

First, we must pray that there be a breaking up of the hard, fallow ground. This is where the church must begin to intercede for nations and for leaders of those nations.

Praying Righteously for Nations

Therefore I exhort first of all that supplications, prayers, intercessions, and giving of thanks be made for all men, for kings and all who are in authority, that we may lead a quiet and peaceable life in all godliness and reverence. For this is good and acceptable in the sight of God our Savior, who desires all men to be saved and to come to the knowledge of the truth.

1 Timothy 2:1–4

We, as the church, must take time and intercede for kings and those in authority. We must ask God to raise up leaders who will make way for the gospel to be preached and to give the church favor. When we pray for this, it doesn't matter who is in authority and leadership, God will move to make this happen. We must not complain and murmur about nations' leaders, but we must pray and intercede for them.

Intercession means to stand in the gap. It means to mediate between two parties. As a member of a nation, and also as a member of the church, we can mediate, or intercede between our nation, and between what God wants to do in that nation. We stand in a place of mediation by taking hold of our nation and its leaders with one hand, and taking hold of our Father and His heart for the harvest of that nation with the other hand, and we ask, petition, and pray for God's will to be done. When we do that, we intercede, and when we intercede, God moves in power!

Pray that the Word Would Have Free Course

> *Finally, brethren, pray for us, that the word of the Lord may run swiftly and be glorified, just as it is with you, and that we may be delivered from unreasonable and wicked men; for not all have faith.*

> **2 Thessalonians 3:1–2**

Another way that we can pray for nations is to pray that there would be no hindrances to the preaching of the gospel. Satan will try to use wicked men and women to try and stop the furtherance of the gospel in a nation. Paul writes to the church in Thessalonica and asks them specifically to pray that the preaching of the Word of God would run swiftly or quickly without hindrances. He lets us know how the word can be hindered by mentioning unreasonable and wicked men.

Can our prayers have an impact on the motives and intentions of these unreasonable and wicked people? Absolutely! Why would the Holy Spirit, through the writings of Paul, ask us to pray if our prayers were not intended to block their evil schemes to stop the Word? As James stated in James 5:16, *"The effective, fervent prayer of a righteous man avails much."* Our prayers cause power to work in those situations.

The Word of God also goes forth in a nation when we pray for God's ministers that are in that nation. God's will open up doors for these ministers to preach the Word in power and demonstration when we pray. These ministers are people, and people get weary, tired, and discouraged at times. We need to pray for their strength and for their boldness to keep preaching the Word of God. The apostle Paul asked the churches at Colossae and at Ephesus to pray for him about this very thing.

"Meanwhile praying also for us, that God would open to us a door for the word, to speak the mystery of Christ, for which I am also in chains" (Col. 4:3).

"And (pray) for me, that utterance may be given to me, that I may open my mouth boldly to make known the mystery of the gospel" (Eph. 6:19).

Many nations that have considered themselves to be "closed" to the preaching of the gospel of Jesus have had supernatural occurrences happen to open up those nations to the gospel. The Soviet Union, along with many other nations that were connected to them by way of communism, was closed for many years to the gospel. The church prayed and the Iron Curtain fell in early 1989. When it fell, the gospel flooded into the former Soviet Union in great power like never before. A harvest continues to be reaped as a result of those prayers being answered.

Germany was another nation that was at one time closed to the gospel of Christ. In November of 1991, the world watched as the great Berlin Wall was torn down. This allowed the gospel to move swiftly into Germany and other nations. German believers testified afterwards that the church in Germany united around praying for a "bloodless revolution" and that is exactly what happened.

We are now seeing God move in nations all over the world as the church takes its place in prayer. What about your nation? Will you pray? Will you be one of the prayer warriors who God uses to bring a mighty move of His Spirit into your nation? Rise up! You are a warrior in the spirit, and when you pray, walls come down! When you pray, mountains move! When you pray, it gives God an entrance into your nation to move because He now has an obedient ambassador who is representing His kingdom, and who is representing your nation. You are interceding, placing your hands on the two parties and bringing the kingdom of heaven into your nation! Hallelujah! Wow!

Acts 4 Praying: Miracles, Signs, and Wonders

One might ask, "But what if a nation persecutes Christians? What if they demand that the gospel be silenced? What if they are even putting Christians to death?" That was the present-day situation in the book of Acts, and the Holy Spirit made sure that we knew exactly how to pray when we find ourselves praying for a nation that is opposed to the gospel of Christ.

In Acts, the church was exploding in growth. This growth was a great threat to national leaders of that day, and those leaders were doing everything in their power to try and stop what God was doing. They were threatening Christians, beating them, and were even stoning them to death. Two of the leaders of the church at that time were Peter and John. Peter and John had been arrested and thrown into jail. What prompted their arrest was the miracle of the healing of the crippled man in Acts 3 when Peter said, "Silver and gold have I none, but such as I have I give you. In the name of Jesus rise and walk!" The miracle caused such chaos and celebration that the authorities arrested Peter and John. They threatened Peter and John and let them go.

What Peter and John did next was the greatest thing that they could have done when being persecuted…they went to a prayer meeting! In Acts 4, they went to their own companions, reported all that had happened, and then they prayed. It is extremely important to note that they all lifted up their voice together, but we have one specific prayer recorded that the Holy Spirit is emphasizing to us. It is a divinely inspired way to pray when persecution is happening.

Notice in the prayer below, they did not pray for the persecution to stop. They did not pray against the rulers and leaders. They prayed for two specific things: boldness and more miracles!

And being let go, they went to their own companions and reported all that the chief priests and elders had said to them. So when they heard that, they raised their voice to God with one accord and said: "Lord, You are God, who made heaven and earth and the sea, and all that is in them, who by the mouth of Your servant David have said: 'Why did the nations rage, and the people plot vain things? The kings of the earth took their stand, and the rulers were gathered together against the Lord and against His Christ.' "For truly against Your holy Servant Jesus, whom You anointed, both Herod and Pontius Pilate, with the Gentiles and the people of Israel, were gathered together to do whatever Your hand and Your purpose determined before to be done. Now, Lord, look on their threats, and grant to Your servants that with all boldness they may speak Your word, by stretching out Your hand to heal, and that signs and wonders may be done through the name of Your holy Servant Jesus." And when they had prayed, the place where they were assembled together was shaken; and they were all filled with the Holy Spirit, and they spoke the word of God with boldness. Now the multitude of those who believed were of one heart and one soul; neither did anyone say that any of the things he possessed was his own, but they had all things in common. And with great power the apostles gave witness to the resurrection of the Lord Jesus. And great grace was upon them all.

Acts 4:23–33

Boldness! More healings, more signs, more wonders! That was the answer that they needed to combat the persecution. What is the devil trying to do in your nation to shut the church down? No matter what he tries to do, the church needs boldness to preach the gospel and demonstrate God's power with signs, wonders, miracles, and healings!

Nations don't need a weak church that bows and compromises to the threats of national leaders. We need boldness to preach and boldness to work miracles in Jesus' name! What would happen in your nation if the church began to boldly give witness to the resurrection of Jesus and many signs and wonders began to be done? You cannot fight darkness with protests or governmental legislation. The only thing that overcomes darkness is light. Light shines when we pray!

THE ARMOR OF GOD

Take Up the Armor...Stand and Pray

Finally, my brethren, be strong in the Lord and in the power of His might. Put on the whole armor of God, that you may be able to stand against the wiles of the devil. For we do not wrestle against flesh and blood, but against principalities, against powers, against the rulers of the darkness of this age, against spiritual hosts of wickedness in the heavenly places. Therefore take up the whole armor of God, that you may be able to withstand in the evil day, and having done all, to stand. Stand therefore, having girded your waist with truth, having put on the breastplate of righteousness, and having shod your feet with the preparation of the gospel of peace; above all, taking the shield of faith with which you will be able to quench all the fiery darts of the wicked one. And take the helmet of salvation, and the sword of the Spirit, which is the word of God; praying always with all prayer and supplication in the Spirit, being watchful

to this end with all perseverance and supplication for
all the saints

Ephesians 6:10–18

In this passage of scripture, the apostle Paul admonishes us to put on spiritual armor that will help us do two things. The first thing this armor helps us to do is to stand against the schemes of the devil.

"Put on the whole armor of God, **that you may be able to stand** *against the wiles of the devil."*

The second thing he tells us to do, after putting this armor on is to pray.

"And take the helmet of salvation, and the sword of the Spirit, which is the word of God...praying."

It is important to notice here that this armor is not our armor, but it is the very armor of God. It is also important to understand the purpose of armor in the time this scripture was written. Back in this time period, armor was worn by soldiers to protect the most vital and vulnerable areas of the body. It was also worn to hold the most important pieces of offensive and defensive weapons of war.

When it comes to standing against the devil, you must have knowledge of his devices and tactics. He doesn't come against us with force or power. He cannot make us sick, or sneak in and kill us. He cannot steal your money or your possessions. The reason he cannot is because over 2,000 years ago Jesus defeated him and stripped him of the power that he had.

The Armor of God

"Having disarmed principalities and powers, He made a public spectacle of them, triumphing over them in it" (Col. 2:15).

"He who sins is of the devil, for the devil has sinned from the beginning. For this purpose the Son of God was manifested, that He might destroy the works of the devil" (1 John 3:8).

Satan's works were destroyed when Jesus was triumphantly raised from the dead. You might ask, "Then why do we need armor to defeat him, if he is already defeated?" The answer is because although he cannot defeat us with force, he will try with deception. Deception is his only tool and weapon. He has been a master of deception from the beginning. Our battle with him is not a physical struggle, but it is a struggle over truth and lies.

He doesn't have the power to make you sick, but he will certainly try to deceive you into believing that you deserve to be sick. He cannot kill you with poverty, but he will try to weigh you down with guilt and condemnation, and deceive you into living a life of poverty because you don't think you deserve to be wealthy. His schemes are to keep people and nations in the dark, and keep them as far away from truth and light as he can. He is a liar, a cheater, and a deceiver, and he has had thousands of years of practice. The good news is with the armor of God, he stands no chance!

"So the great dragon was cast out, that serpent of old, called the Devil and Satan, who deceives the whole world; he was cast to the earth, and his angels were cast out with him" (Rev. 12:9).

"But I fear, lest somehow, as the serpent deceived Eve by his craftiness, so your minds may be corrupted from the simplicity that is in Christ" (2 Cor. 11:3).

"And the LORD God said to the woman, 'What is this you have done?' The woman said, 'The serpent deceived me, *and I ate'"* (Gen. 3:13).

Since our battle with him is over truth and deception, then that's exactly what the armor pertains to. Each piece of the armor is a revelation of vital truth that you must have in order to stand and pray effectively. If armor protects the most vital areas of a soldier's body, then the armor of God is truth that protects you in the most vital areas of deception. Let's look at each piece and how each piece empowers and helps us to stand and pray.

Pray with Your Belt On

"Stand therefore, having girded your waist with truth" (Eph. 6:14).

Back in this time period a soldier wore a belt. The purpose of the belt was to be a central place where all the armor tied together. It also served the purpose of holding the sheath of the sword, and perhaps other weapons. It would be one of the first things that a soldier would put on. Paul calls this piece of God's armor the "belt of truth."

There are many truths that we could talk about here. The truth about who God really is. The truth about who we are in Him. The truth about our adversary and so on. Since we are talking about the most vital truth upon which all truth is built, let's talk about the truth of Jesus, the cornerstone of all truth, and the foundation upon which all truth is built.

In order to stand effectively, and in order to pray effectively, we must be grounded in the truth of who Jesus is, why He came, and what He did on our behalf. Jesus is God, who emptied Himself and came to this earth as a man, to redeem us from sin's power and show us what a man filled with God looks like and how he operates. He died on the cross, paying the full payment of man's sin debt. After the full payment was made, He was raised from the dead, securing our justification. Because of Jesus, we are redeemed and justified. Because of what He did, we are healed and free. When we believe on Him, everything that He secured for us becomes ours by grace through faith. Because of Jesus, we now stand in the abundance of His finished work.

After He was raised from the dead, He ascended to the Father and sat down at His right hand until all His enemies become His footstool. He will return to the earth as the scripture teaches and set up His kingdom physically on this earth. He will reign forever as King of kings and Lord of lords. This is Jesus whom we preach.

We can assume that everyone is established in the knowledge of who Jesus is, but that would be a catastrophic assumption. We must have the knowledge of Him first. This knowledge is the first piece of armor that to which all other armor is tied to. It is the most central part of the armor that holds all weapons that we fight with. Without this knowledge, you cannot stand against the devil, for it was Jesus who defeated him with His finished work. Without this knowledge, there is no need to pray and no legal ground of redemption upon which to base our prayers on. The knowledge of Jesus is the belt of truth!

And I, brethren, when I came to you, did not come with excellence of speech or of wisdom declaring to you the testimony of God. For I determined not to know anything among you except Jesus Christ and Him crucified.

1 Corinthians 2:1–2

"*who was delivered up because of our offenses, and was raised because of our justification*" (Rom. 4:25).

"*and by Him everyone who believes is justified from all things from which you could not be justified by the law of Moses*" (Acts 13:39).

And without controversy great is the mystery of godliness: God was manifested in the flesh, justified in the Spirit, seen by angels, preached among the Gentiles, believed on in the world, received up in glory.

1 Timothy 3:16

"*For there is one God and one Mediator between God*

and men, the Man Christ Jesus" (1 Tim. 2:5).

> *And while they looked steadfastly toward heaven as*
> *He went up, behold, two men stood by them in white*
> *apparel, who also said, "Men of Galilee, why do you*
> *stand gazing up into heaven? This same Jesus, who*
> *was taken up from you into heaven, will so come in*
> *like manner as you saw Him go into heaven."*
>
> **Acts 1:10–11**

Jesus is God, manifested in the flesh, sinless in His virgin birth, the model of all Christian life and ministry, the payment for our sin, the healing of our sickness, the crucified lamb of God, the resurrected champion, the mediator at the Father's right hand, the coming King of the kingdom, and His reign will never end!

Pray with Your Breastplate On

...having put on the breastplate of righteousness

Since we have covered righteousness in great detail in "Pray Like a Righteous Man," we won't spend a lot of time on this piece of armor, but let us recognize one thing of great importance. This piece of armor covers areas of the body, that if wounded, would prove deadly.

The breastplate covers the heart, the lungs, and other vital organs. If deception comes in the area of your righteousness, you would certainly be defeated. We have to wear the knowledge of our righteousness that is given to us by faith, like a soldier wears his breastplate. We don't stand in our own righteousness, we stand in the gift of righteousness that is given to us at the new birth. It is the very righteousness of Jesus Christ. We stand in that righteousness that cannot be moved. That righteousness defeated the devil once (once and for all) and when we hold up the righteousness of Jesus in prayer, it is a banner of victory over everything the devil could try to do.

I don't pray from the basis of my righteousness, and how holy I am in my performance. I pray as a righteous man in Christ. I pray as Jesus prayed, with the same power and authority, because I have His right standing. The devil cannot deceive me by saying, "God will not hear and answer your prayers because you have done things wrong!" If he tries that I just say, "Devil, I don't pray in my name, I pray in Jesus' name! I don't stand in my righteousness, I stand in Jesus' righteousness because He gave it to me! Now flee in Jesus' name!" Wear your righteousness like a breastplate! Stand right and pray!

Pray with You Shoes On!

...and having shod your feet with the preparation of the gospel of peace

Peace means to be exempt of (free from) chaos and war. It's a state we're in because of Jesus. Without the peace that

He made between us and God, there is enmity (or hostility). Without Jesus, our relationship with God is broken, and there always seems to be something missing, something not quite right.

Because of Jesus, we now enjoy a relationship with God where nothing is missing, and nothing is broken. When we approach God, He's smiling. There are not hidden feelings of disappointment that He has for us because now He sees us in Christ. When we approach God in prayer, it is as if Jesus is approaching the Father because we come to the Father in Jesus' name.

Shoes are something you put on before you walk somewhere, therefore, when we come to God in prayer, we need to have put on shoes of peace. We come into His presence knowing He hears us and welcomes our petitions. We come with confidence, knowing He hears us and grants us the petitions we are asking of Him. He is delighted we are there, and He delights in what we have to say.

> *Now this is the confidence that we have in Him, that if we ask anything according to His will, He hears us. And if we know that He hears us, whatever we ask, we know that we have the petitions that we have asked of Him.*

1 John 5:14–15

It is also important to understand this peace we have with God when it comes to praying for other believers, for they have this peace too. When we pray for them, we pray that their eyes would be opened to this relationship of peace that they have with the Father though Jesus.

Peace also causes us to be bold in our asking. We should not be afraid to ask the Lord for big things, for He is a big God who loves us and delights in our prosperity. There was a story told of a king who had a vast domain. His riches were beyond words and his kingdom was huge and magnificent. One day, as different people were coming before him with request, a lowly citizen walked into his court and asked something so big, so enormous, that the king's subjects around the throne laughed and mocked the man for asking such a thing of the great king. The subjects nearly fainted when the king granted the man his petition. As the man turned and walked away, the subjects asked the king why he would grant the man such a request. The king's reply was, "The enormity of his request honored me."

In other words, the man asked such a huge thing of the king, because he believed the king was big enough to do it. Big asking and big faith honored the king. Do we, as believers serve a big God? Do we believe His resources never run out and He always has more than enough? Do we believe we have peace with our King through Jesus? Then why are you asking so small? Give God a request that will honor Him. You have peace with the God of the universe, and you are a son of His through Jesus. Let peace move you to pray boldly and ask big!

Pray with Your Shield Up!

...above all, taking the shield of faith with which you will be able to quench all the fiery darts of the wicked one.

Thoughts come to us all, and they come to us all the time. Some thoughts are godly, and when we allow those thoughts to enter our heart, they produce peace and joy. Some thoughts are not godly, and if we let them in, they produce fear, condemnation, guilt, shame, and all sorts of death. These thoughts that are from the enemy are called "fiery darts." Why? Because when they hit us, they burn with destruction.

The enemy's fiery darts come in the form of thoughts, suggestions, and ideas. Remember, he is a master of deceit, so he must try and appeal to your logic and your reasoning. Fiery darts don't have a sign hanging on them that says, "This is from the devil!" They are more subtle. If the devil wanted to try and get you to steal something, he wouldn't just say to you, "Hey, why don't you steal that?" He would appeal to your logic. He would say "If you take that, no one will ever know. They really don't need it and they probably really don't want it anyway. Besides that, they will never notice that it's gone."

Sounds logical doesn't it? But watch out...there is fire attached to that logic! Notice how he tempted Adam and Eve in the very beginning. Notice the logical thoughts, suggestions, and ideas:

Now the serpent was more cunning than any beast of

the field which the Lord God had made. And he said to the woman, "Has God indeed said, 'You shall not eat of every tree of the garden'?" And the woman said to the serpent, "We may eat the fruit of the trees of the garden; but of the fruit of the tree which is in the midst of the garden, God has said, 'You shall not eat it, nor shall you touch it, lest you die.'" Then the serpent said to the woman, "You will not surely die. For God knows that in the day you eat of it your eyes will be opened, and you will be like God, knowing good and evil." So when the woman saw that the tree was good for food, that it was pleasant to the eyes, and a tree desirable to make one wise, she took of its fruit and ate. She also gave to her husband with her, and he ate. Then the eyes of both of them were opened, and they knew that they were naked; and they sewed fig leaves together and made themselves coverings.

Genesis 3:1–7

What could Eve have done in this situation? She could have held up her shield of faith. Her shield of faith were the beliefs she had as a result of what God had told her. Instead quenching the fiery darts of the devil, she tried to reason things out in her mind. Because her shield was down, the fiery darts got in and death was the result.

So when it comes to the fiery darts that are aimed at our lives, how can we know if our shield is up, or if it is down? By always asking ourselves the question, "What has God said about this?" Our shield of faith is our beliefs that we have as a result of what God has said to us. Those beliefs acts as a filter, allowing godly thoughts to enter, and rejecting the fiery thoughts before they hit.

When we gain the knowledge of God's word, it gives us faith. Without knowing what He said, you have no faith. Faith cannot exist in your heart unless you first know what God has said.

"So then faith comes by hearing, and hearing by the word of God" (Rom. 10:17).

If you don't know what He said about a certain thing, you have no faith in that area. If you have no faith in an area, you have no shield in that area. If you have no shield, then deceptive, fiery darts are able to get in because you don't have the means to extinguish them.

Here's an example. Suppose I wanted to begin to invest my money in the business of importing and exporting goods, and let's also suppose you were an expert at import/export, and suppose you have been doing this business all your life. You have much knowledge of this business and your experience has caused you to be very successful. I have no knowledge, so I attend a two-hour seminar on the business of import/export. Now suppose I come to you and begin to persuade you to listen to me and my expert advice. After all,

I know everything I need to know because I have attended the two-hour seminar. I begin to use logical thoughts, suggestions, and ideas to try and get you to invest money in my new business.

What is going to happen in you as I begin to share my suggestions and ideas? Something is going to rise within you. What is it? It is all the knowledge you have gained through a lifetime of experience. Why, you wouldn't listen to me. You would immediately begin to reject my suggestions and recognize that I am someone that you shouldn't trust with your money! What would give you the ability to do that? Your shield of faith that you have developed by all the knowledge and experience you have. If you didn't have that shield, I could possibly swindle money from you and persuade you to agree with me. Because you have knowledge, you now have a shield to allow truthful thoughts and reject false ones.

I have a strong shield of faith when it comes to certain areas, but my shield could be weak in areas where I have no knowledge. When we study God's word and get our hearts established in His promises, it gives us a shield to stop the enemies fiery darts. You need this shield when it comes to prayer. As you pray, petitioning the Father and interceding for your nation, the enemy will try to stop you with thoughts, suggestions, and ideas. He will say things like, "God won't answer that prayer!" Or he will say, "Your nation will never change. It's too corrupt, and it has been this way for many, many years!" Your faith in what God has said will cause you to raise your shield and stop those discouraging, fiery darts.

The shield of faith, when held up, can cause us to continue to pray and not lose heart. It can cause us to stop what the enemy is doing, and not give him the opportunity to deceive us. Find out what God has said, and then hold that shield up. Stand with that shield. Stand right and pray!

Pray with Your Helmet On

...And take the helmet of salvation

We must stand and pray with the knowledge of our salvation. We are saved because we have believed on Jesus and confessed Him as Lord of our lives. We are not just saved from hell, and we are not just saved from sin. Our salvation is much bigger than that!

> *That if you confess with your mouth the Lord Jesus and believe in your heart that God has raised Him from the dead, you will be saved. For with the heart one believes unto righteousness, and with the mouth confession is made unto salvation.*

Romans 10:9–10

The word "saved" in Romans 10:9 is the Greek word *sozo*. The word "salvation" in verse 10 is the Greek word *soteria*, and they both mean the same thing. Here is their meaning from the Greek:

- To save, keep safe and sound, to rescue from danger

or destruction.

- To save a suffering one from perishing or from disease.

- To make well, heal, and restore to health.

- To deliver from the penalties of judgment.

- To save from the evils which obstruct the reception of the Messianic deliverance

As you can see, this is much more than being saved from hell and sin. We are saved from hell and we are saved from sin, but our salvation includes deliverance, healing, protection, safety, soundness, and rescue. We are saved! We have salvation! We need to have this knowledge in order to stand and pray. We can pray with authority when we know these rights and privileges that are ours in Christ.

Pray with Your Sword

...and the sword of the Spirit, which is the word of God

The shield is our defense, but the sword is used in offensive warfare. We hold up the shield to stop the enemy's attack, but we use the sword to make progress, to push the enemy back and to defeat him. When we pray, we need to accurately use the Word of God like a soldier accurately handles his sword.

Jesus used this same sword against the devil when he attacked Him in the wilderness. He both stopped the fiery darts, and He defeated the devil with the knowledge of the

Word of God. He is our example, and we do battle the same way He did. We use the Word of God like a sword.

Then Jesus, being filled with the Holy Spirit, returned from the Jordan and was led by the Spirit into the wilderness, being tempted for forty days by the devil. And in those days He ate nothing, and afterward, when they had ended, He was hungry. And the devil said to Him, "If You are the Son of God, command this stone to become bread." But Jesus answered him, saying, "It is written, 'Man shall not live by bread alone, but by every word of God.'" Then the devil, taking Him up on a high mountain, showed Him all the kingdoms of the world in a moment of time. And the devil said to Him, "All this authority I will give You, and their glory; for this has been delivered to me, and I give it to whomever I wish. Therefore, if You will worship before me, all will be Yours." And Jesus answered and said to him, "Get behind Me, Satan! For it is written, 'You shall worship the Lord your God, and Him only you shall serve.'" Then he brought Him to Jerusalem, set Him on the pinnacle of the temple, and said to Him, "If You are the Son of God, throw Yourself down from here. For it is writ-

ten: 'He shall give His angels charge over you, to keep you,' and, 'In their hands they shall bear you up, lest you dash your foot against a stone.'" And Jesus answered and said to him, "It has been said, 'You shall not tempt the Lord your God.'" Now when the devil had ended every temptation, he departed from Him until an opportune time.

Luke 4:1–13

Notice the logical thoughts, suggestions and ideas that the devil used like darts. Jesus stopped those fiery darts with the knowledge He had of the Word of God. He also took the Word of God and wielded it like a sword. Every time He stated "It is written," He was pulling out His sword and driving back the enemy. What was the result? The enemy left Him! Why? The devil cannot stop the Word of God. The Word of God is the most powerful utterance that exists!

For the word of God is living and powerful, and sharper than any two-edged sword, piercing even to the division of soul and spirit, and of joints and marrow, and is a discerner of the thoughts and intents of the heart.

Hebrews 4:12

The Armor of God

The armor of God is extremely important when it comes to prayer. In fact, one of the main reasons the scripture tells us to put it on is to pray. It causes us to pray effectively, just like a soldier, who cannot be effective in battle without it. The armor is revelation knowledge of who we are and what we have, established in our heart, for the purpose of standing and for the purpose of praying.

"Finally, my brethren, be strong in the Lord and in the power of His might. Put on the whole armor of God, that you may be able to stand against the wiles of the devil...Praying!" (Eph. 6:10–11,18a).

COMMANDING ANGELS

Angels, Our Servants

You might be wondering why a book on the subject of prayer has a chapter on angels. The reason is because angels play an important role in answered prayers being answered. We are not to commune with angels, worship angels or pray to angels, but we need to know how we interact with these beings that God has created, and what role they play in our lives, since we are created beings, too.

The scripture has many things to say about angels. Angels are mentioned around 300 times in the Bible. Here are a few things the scripture tells us about them:

Their number is innumerable.

"But you have come to Mount Zion and to the city of the living God, the heavenly Jerusalem, to an innumerable company of angels" (Heb. 12:22).

They are mighty in strength and carry out the words of God.

"Bless the Lord, you His angels, who excel in strength, who do His word, heeding the voice of His word" (Ps.103:20).

Angels are an entirely different order of being than humans. Human beings do not become angels

after they die. Angels will never become, and never were, human beings. God created the angels

just as He created humanity. Nowhere does the Bible state that angels are created in the image and likeness of God, as humans are. Angels are spiritual beings that can, to a certain degree, take on physical form as they did in some instances in the scriptures, both in the Old and New Testament. The greatest thing we can learn from the holy angels is their instant, unquestioning obedience to God's commands.

Because angels are huge, strong beings, many people believed they were created with a higher, more superior place than men. Many men upon seeing angels have been filled with fear, fainted, and even attempted to worship them. The apostle Paul warned the New Testament church against the worship of angels:

"Let no one cheat you of your reward, taking delight in false humility and worship of angels, intruding into those things which he has not seen, vainly puffed up by his fleshly mind" (Col. 2:18).

When we look at what the scripture says, we find that angels were not created superior to man, but just the opposite…they serve man. Look at what Psalm 8 says about the creation of man.

"What is man that You are mindful of him, and the son of man that You visit him? For You have made him a little lower than the angels, and You have crowned him with glory and honor" (Ps. 8:4–5).

This scripture seems to say that man was created lower than the angels, but the Hebrew word that is translated "angels" in verse 5 is the Hebrew word "Elohim." *Elohim* is not the word for angels, but is the name for God Himself. Then why would the translators put the word angels? Perhaps they could not fathom that man is superior to beings that are extremely powerful and majestic in appearance?

This is why it's important to study the word thoroughly and compare scripture with other scripture. The rank of God's creation is not angels first, then man is placed under angels. The rank is God, then man, then angels underneath man. Let's look at a few other scriptures that give insight into the place of angels.

"Are they (angels) not all ministering spirits sent forth to minister for those who will inherit salvation?" (Heb. 1:14).

According to this scripture, angels are ministering spirits. The word minister means to serve. Angels are *serving spirits*. Spirits that wait on and serve. Who do they serve? They serve God, but this scripture says they are ministers, or servants, "for those who are heirs of salvation." They are servants and ministers to the body of Christ, the heirs of salvation.

> *And I fell at his feet to worship him. But he said to me, "See that you do not do that! I am your fellow servant, and of your brethren who have the testimony of Jesus. Worship God! For the testimony of Jesus is the spirit of prophecy."*
>
> **Revelation 19:10**

Now I, John, saw and heard these things. And when I heard and saw, I fell down to worship before the feet of the angel who showed me these things. Then he said to me, "See that you do not do that. For I am your fellow servant, and of your brethren the prophets, and of those who keep the words of this book. Worship God."

Revelation 22:8–9

Here in the book of Revelation, John was so caught up in the awe of the angels' presence that he began to worship the angel. This angel, as all angels do, prohibited (stopped or forbid) John from worshipping him and pointed John's worship to God. Notice what the angel told John. He said he was John's servant and a servant of all those who obey God.

You see, angels are servants to God and to man. One way they serve us is in carrying out the words of God. When we pray according to God's word, angels go to work to bring the words of God to pass. They hearken to the words of God.

Aid to the Heirs

We see many places in the Bible where angels brought things from God's presence to give aid to people. In the book of Daniel as Daniel was seeking the Lord, an angel appeared to him bringing a message from God concerning the nation of Israel, and with the message he brought divine ability to understand.

Now while I was speaking, praying, and confessing my sin and the sin of my people Israel, and presenting my supplication before the Lord my God for the holy mountain of my God, yes, while I was speaking in prayer, the man Gabriel, whom I had seen in the vision at the beginning, being caused to fly swiftly, reached me about the time of the evening offering. And he informed me, and talked with me, and said, "O Daniel, I have now come forth to give you skill to understand."

Daniel 9:20–22

The angel brought a divine message, and he brought with it skill to understand it. Angels brought messages in the New Testament also. This is important to understand, because it tells us that angels can still bring messages to us today, since we are still living under the same covenant and in the same dispensation.

There was a certain man in Caesarea called Cornelius, a centurion of what was called the Italian Regiment, a devout man and one who feared God with all his household, who gave alms generously to the people, and prayed to God always. About the ninth hour of the day he saw clearly in a vision an angel of God coming in and saying to him, "Cornelius!" And when he observed him, he was afraid, and said, "What is it, lord?" So he said to him, "Your prayers and your alms have come up for a memorial before God. Now send men to Joppa, and send for Simon whose surname is Peter. He is lodging with Simon, a tanner, whose house is by the sea. He will tell you what you must do."

Acts 10:1–6

The angel in the vision gave Cornelius a message and directed him to Peter so the Gentiles could find out how to be saved. Guidance came by way of an angel.

But after long abstinence from food, then Paul stood in the midst of them and said, "Men, you should have listened to me, and not have sailed from Crete and incurred this disaster and loss. And now I urge you to take heart, for there will be no loss of life among you, but only of the ship. For there stood by me this night an angel of the God to whom I belong and whom I serve, saying, 'Do not be afraid, Paul; you must be brought before Caesar; and indeed God has granted you all those who sail with you.'"

Acts 27:21–24

Commanding Angels

The apostle Paul was given a message of hope that all the men on the ship would survive a horrific storm that they were encountering. Angels can encourage us with a message of hope.

Angels are ministers of aid to the people of God. They can bring a message, understanding, divine protection, and they can also bring strength. Here is an instance where angels ministered to Jesus as He was praying in the garden. They aided Him by bringing Him strength during an intense time of prayer:

And He was withdrawn from them about a stone's throw, and He knelt down and prayed, saying, "Father, if it is Your will, take this cup away from Me; nevertheless not My will, but Yours, be done." Then an angel appeared to Him from heaven, strengthening Him. And being in agony, He prayed more earnestly. Then His sweat became like great drops of blood falling down to the ground.

Luke 22:41–44

If angels ministered this way to the early church and to Jesus, then we should expect that the same thing can happen to us as we do the will of the Father in the earth. Expect the help of heaven's armies of angels when you need it most. They bring aid to the heirs!

Directing the Armies

God is always a God of order and never the author of confusion. We always see order and rank in His creation. There is even a heavenly rank of authority in the Godhead. Jesus said that the Father is greater than all. He also said that the Son is subject to the Father. The heavenly rank we see in the Godhead is Father, Son, and Holy Spirit. We see a rank in the angelic realm. We see seraphim, cherubim, and archangels. We also see rank in the body of Christ with offices like apostles, prophets, pastors, evangelists, and teachers. As we have seen earlier, man is not created inferior to angels. Angels are to serve the church. They help to carry out God's plan and His great commission of preaching the gospel in the earth.

If angels are to serve us, then we must direct them as to what to do. We cannot just direct them to do whatever we want them to do, but we command them to do the will of the Lord, revealed to us in His word. Remember, they hearken unto the word of the Lord. They will obey that word and aid us in the advancing of God's kingdom. They aid us in bringing God's promises to pass. If we need finances for God's work, we don't ask God to give us money. Money isn't made in heaven. If God made money and gave it to us, it would be counterfeit. Money is here on earth and God knows how to get it to us. So how do we pray in a way that involves the help of angels?

First, since God has already promised to meet our every need, we must claim whatever we need by faith. Second, we tell the devil to take his hands off of our money and

God's money. We bind him from hindering and holding up this money in Jesus' name. Third, we say to the ministering spirits or angels, "Go now and bring in the money that I have claimed. The money that belongs to God's kingdom and to us!" Once we have prayed this way, there is no need to pray about it anymore. From then on we just praise and thank God that the money is coming in and that we will have every need met.

Here's another example: If we are praying for our nation, we know certain things that God wants for our nation. He wants righteousness. He wants justice. He wants the leaders to make decisions that would aid His kingdom spreading and advancing. So when we pray for our leaders and intercede for our nation, we can command angels to go forth and bring influence and change in our nation according to the will of the Father.

Therefore I exhort first of all that supplications, prayers, intercessions, and giving of thanks be made for all men, for kings and all who are in authority, that we may lead a quiet and peaceable life in all godliness and reverence. For this is good and acceptable in the sight of God our Savior, who desires all men to be saved and to come to the knowledge of the truth.

1 Timothy 2:1–4

Stand Right and Pray

You can take this scripture, which reveals God's will to us, and pray for your nation like this:

"Father, in the name of Jesus, I pray for my country on the behalf of all the men and women in it. I thank You that your desire is to work in this country, and that all men would be saved and come to the knowledge of the truth that is in Jesus.

"I pray for all of the leaders who make decisions about this country. I pray that they would make decisions that would to further the kingdom of God. I pray that they would make decisions that would result in peace, godliness, and reverence. Raise up leaders who would favor your church and your kingdom.

"I take authority now over the devil and all his host of demons that are trying to destroy the church and hinder it. I bind you now, demons, in the mighty name of Jesus, and I command your work to stop. Persecution...Stop! Favor...begin!

"And now I speak to the ministering spirits, the angels of my God, go now and bring these prayers to

pass! Go and influence for righteousness, justice, and peace! Go and aid the church in a harvest of souls for God's kingdom! Hallelujah!"

PRAYING IN OTHER TONGUES

The Baptism in the Holy Spirit

The New Testament letters to churches, from the book of Acts all the way to Revelation, were written presupposing that the reader has had two vital experiences in their life. First, it is written presupposing that the reader has been born again, receiving the salvation experience that God offers the world through what Jesus did in His death, burial, and resurrection. This is the first experience an unbeliever must have. Second, it is written presupposing that the reader has experienced the baptism in the Holy Spirit, a subsequent experience that Jesus has for every person that would believe on Him.

Jesus first spoke of the importance of the baptism in the Holy Spirit in the beginning of the book of Acts. The disciples had been born again by believing on the resurrected Christ and had received the Holy Spirit when Jesus breathed on them in John 20.

"So Jesus said to them again, 'Peace to you! As the Father has sent Me, I also send you.' And when He had said this, He breathed on them, and said to them, 'Receive the

Holy Spirit "" (John 20:21–22).

When the disciples received the Holy Spirit, they were born again. At salvation, the Holy Spirit comes to abide in us and gives us new life. We receive the life-giving Spirit of God and He dwells in us to be our helper and our guide in all things that pertain to life and godliness. The Holy Spirit dwells in a born-again believer, but just because someone has experienced this first experience, does not mean they have received the second experience. The first experience of salvation is when we are born of the Spirit. It is an inflow of the Spirit coming from God toward us and bringing salvation. The second experience of the baptism in the Holy Spirit is when He flows out of us in power and anoints us to demonstrate the power of God as a witness to the world. It is an outflow of the Spirit from within us.

"But you shall receive power when the Holy Spirit has come upon you; and you shall be witnesses to Me in Jerusalem, and in all Judea and Samaria, and to the end of the earth" (Acts 1:8).

Jesus spoke here concerning the second Holy Spirit experience. The people He was talking to had already received the first experience. The first experience was for them. The second experience was to equip them to be witnesses to the world.

This second experience was so vital that Jesus would not allow them to leave the upper room until they had received it. It was the power that they needed to accomplish what He was sending them to do. This experience was not only for them and the early church. It was for all who would believe after them. That includes you and me!

"*For the promise is to you and to your children, and to all who are afar off, as many as the Lord our God will call*" (Acts 2:39).

Salvation and baptism in the Holy Spirit are two separate encounters, but they are not optional encounters. We cannot choose one and deny the other. The same Holy Spirit that saves you and comes to dwell in you wants to fill you and flow out of you in a supernatural way. You cannot say, "I want salvation but I don't want the baptism in the Holy Spirit." To be a part of the church of Jesus Christ you need both. You need the first Holy Spirit experience to save you and to make you a part of His church. You need the second to empower and equip you to be His church and to represent Him in the way He wants to be represented: supernaturally with the power of the Spirit flowing out of you. He has always expected His kingdom to go forth in the power of the Spirit with miracles, healings, signs, and wonders.

"*For the kingdom of God is not in word but in power*" (1 Cor. 4:20).

And I, brethren, when I came to you, did not come with excellence of speech or of wisdom declaring to you the testimony of God. For I determined not to know anything among you except Jesus Christ and Him crucified. I was with you in weakness, in fear, and in much trembling. And my speech and my preaching were not with persuasive words of human wisdom, but in demonstration of the Spirit and of power, that your faith should not be in the wisdom of men but in the power of God.

1 Corinthians 2:1–5

We have seen both experiences spoken of and at work in the first disciples of Jesus after His resurrection. As the church grew, we see both experiences at work in the believers that followed. In Acts 8, the evangelist Philip went to a city called Samaria, where amazing things happened. The power of God flowed through Philip. The Holy Spirit was not only in Philip, He was flowing out of him just as Jesus said in miracles and signs and wonders. The result was a city-wide move of God where multitudes were born again. Multitudes received the first experience of salvation, but we also see the urgency of the church in Jerusalem to send Peter and John so they could receive the second experience.

Therefore those who were scattered went everywhere preaching the word. Then Philip went down to the city of Samaria and preached Christ to them. And the multitudes with one accord heeded the things spoken by Philip, hearing and seeing the miracles which he did. For unclean spirits, crying with a loud voice, came out of many who were possessed; and many

who were paralyzed and lame were healed. And there
was great joy in that city.

Acts 8:4–8

Verse 6 says the multitude "heeded the things spoken by
Philip" which means they were born again by believing the
gospel that Philip preached. Being born again is great, but
there's another experience that believers need.

Now when the apostles who were at Jerusalem heard
that Samaria had received the word of God, they sent
Peter and John to them, who, when they had come
down, prayed for them that they might receive the
Holy Spirit. For as yet He had fallen upon none of
them. They had only been baptized in the name of the
Lord Jesus. Then they laid hands on them, and they
received the Holy Spirit.

Acts 8:14–17

Verse 16 says these believers had been baptized in the
name of Jesus, which means they had been born again and
saved, but they had not received the second experience that
the first Christians had received in Acts 2. When Peter and
John laid hands on them, they received the second experience. Just like in the first believers experienced, these Sa-

maritan believers spoke with tongues supernaturally. How do you know? Because Simon the sorcerer, who was not a believer, *saw* that through the laying on of the disciples' hands, the Holy Spirit was given and he wanted that ability because he knew he could make money with something that powerful.

> *And when Simon saw that through the laying on of the apostles' hands the Holy Spirit was given, he offered them money, saying, "Give me this power also, that anyone on whom I lay hands may receive the Holy Spirit." But Peter said to him, "Your money perish with you, because you thought that the gift of God could be purchased with money! You have neither part nor portion in this matter, for your heart is not right in the sight of God. Repent therefore of this your wickedness, and pray God if perhaps the thought of your heart may be forgiven you. For I see that you are poisoned by bitterness and bound by iniquity." Then Simon answered and said, "Pray to the Lord for me, that none of the things which you have spoken may come upon me."*
>
> ***Acts 8:18–24***

The Biblical evidence that confirms that people received the second experience of the baptism in the Holy Spirit is that they spoke in other tongues. Speaking in other tongues is the first thing that happens when you receive this baptism by faith. He flows out of you with a heavenly prayer language. Remember, salvation is an inflow…the baptism in the Holy Spirit is an outflow! Here is another encounter where we see the two experiences at work in people:

> *And it happened, while Apollos was at Corinth, that Paul, having passed through the upper regions, came to Ephesus. And finding some disciples he said to them, "Did you receive the Holy Spirit when you believed?" So they said to him, "We have not so much as heard whether there is a Holy Spirit." And he said to them, "Into what then were you baptized?" So they said, "Into John's baptism." Then Paul said, "John indeed baptized with a baptism of repentance, saying to the people that they should believe on Him who would come after him, that is, on Christ Jesus." When they heard this, they were baptized in the name of the Lord Jesus. And when Paul had laid hands on them, the Holy Spirit came upon them, and they spoke with tongues and prophesied. Now the men were about twelve in all.*

Acts 19:1–7

Two experiences. First, in verse 5, they believed Paul's preaching and were baptized in the name of the Lord Jesus. This means they were born again and received the first experience. Then, when Paul laid his hands on them, they were baptized in the Holy Spirit and the outflow began... they spoke with tongues and prophesied!

When God Prays Through Us

Tongues is, and needs to be, a critically important part of our prayer life. Our need for tongues is simply stated in the book of Romans 8.

"Likewise the Spirit also helps in our weaknesses. For we do not know what we should pray for as we ought, but the Spirit Himself makes intercession for us with groanings which cannot be uttered" (Rom. 8:26).

Here is the weakness that we all have that makes praying in tongues so important: "We do not know what we should pray for as we ought." We are humans and our understanding is seriously limited when compared to God's. He knows everything about everyone. He knows details that we could never know. He knows the very thoughts and intentions of a person's heart. We could never know that. So when it comes to praying for people, we really don't know how to pray effectively.

That's why we need the baptism in the Holy Spirit with ability to pray in other tongues. When we pray in tongues, the Holy Spirit is praying through us with accurate perfection! Have you ever wanted to pray for someone, but you didn't know where to start? We all have. That's the weakness that this verse is talking about. Praying in tongues is allowing the Holy Spirit to pray and intercede through you with groanings and words that cannot be uttered in your own language that you understand. It is prayer beyond your understanding. It is prayer that taps into the perfect understanding of the Holy Spirit.

"Now He who searches the hearts knows what the mind of the Spirit is, because He makes intercession for the saints according to the will of God" (Rom. 8:27).

When you pray in tongues, the Holy Spirit is interceding through you "according to the will of God." You never have to worry that you are praying something wrong when you pray in tongues. You are yielding your vocal chords to Him and allowing Him to use them to pray exactly what needs to be prayed. What an amazing gift!

Dual Blessings: Charging Your Battery While Praying Mysteries

What happens when a person speaks in tongues is described in 1 Corinthians 14. Paul describes two of the many things that happen when we pray in tongues.

"For he who speaks in a tongue does not speak to men but to God, for no one understands him; however, in the spirit he speaks mysteries. He who speaks in a tongue edifies himself" (1 Cor. 14:2, 4a).

When you speak in tongues, your prayer is directed to

God. No one understands it, not you, not the devil…only God! It's a direct line from your spirit to the heart of God, overseen and managed by the Holy Spirit Himself. Verse 2 says you speak mysteries, which means "things outside the realm of your understanding and intelligence." Sounds like Romans 8:26! We have the ability to pray things that we cannot comprehend or figure out. Things that are mysteries to us, but not to God.

Another thing that happens when you pray in tongues is that you "edify yourself." The word edify means "to charge" much like the way you would charge a battery. Many times in life, I would dare to even say daily, we need to be edified, or charged up. When you pray in tongues this is what's happening. A charged battery is one that functions at a maximum capacity. It's charge affects all the things that are connected to it. That battery is responsible for bringing power to everything it touches, so it needs to be functioning at full capacity.

As an ambassador of the kingdom of God, our job is to bring the power of His kingdom to everyone we meet, everywhere we go. We need to be functioning at full capacity everywhere we go. When we pray in tongues we edify ourselves, and build ourselves up so that we are a ready vessel for God to use. Praying in other tongues prepares us to stay yielded to the Holy Spirit as we go in His power. We are ready at all times to release our faith to help humanity around us. When you yield to the Holy Spirit and pray in tongues, it helps you stay ready in faith!

"But you, beloved, building yourselves up on your most holy faith, praying in the Holy Spirit" (Jude 1:20).

Being Led By The Spirit In Prayer

We should not only expect the Holy Spirit to help us pray when we pray in other tongues, but we should expect Him to lead us at all times when we pray. Prayer should be a journey of following the Holy Spirit. It's a fun and exciting journey that's never dull or monotonous when He is helping us and leading us.

"Praying always with all prayer and supplication in the Spirit, being watchful to this end with all perseverance and supplication for all the saints" (Eph. 6:18).

How can you effectively pray for all saints? The answer is "in the Spirit!" If you look at the original Greek language here in this verse, it actually says to pray "being led by the Spirit." Whether we are praying in tongues, or praying with our understanding, we should allow the Holy Spirit to lead us.

A great way to illustrate this is think of prayer as a river, and think of your prayer life as if you are paddling down that river in a boat. Sometimes the river is peaceful and easy. As you paddle in this peaceful river, you come around a turn of the river and the water changes. Maybe there's faster water that turns into a rushing adventure. The speed picks up as you navigate the turns. As you paddle on, the river might get quiet and peaceful again, but then it might change as you round the next turn. You are not in control of the river, you are simply navigating to stay in the middle of it.

That's how it is to pray, being led by the Spirit. He's the river and you are navigating to be in His flow. As you pray, you are listening to Him and sensing His heart and you are following His cues. You may start out praying in worship to the Father. Then, you might sense that He is leading you to pray in other tongues for a while. After you have done that, you might sense the river slow down and go back to worship. Then He might lead you to pray for an individual, or a group of people, or your nation. You might sense Him lead you to make prophetic declarations of the Word of God over your nation and leaders, and as you do, you might sense Him leading you back to praying in other tongues, this time with more fervency because the river is changing. He has moved you from worship to intercession as you follow His lead.

Don't make prayer boring by praying the same way all the time. Follow His lead and paddle down the river. Sense His heart and let Him lead you down the river. As you do tremendous result will follow. Your prayers will become life-transforming and nation-shaking!

STAY WITH IT!

Don't Stop Until You Are Done

Prayer is not a duty that we are obligated to perform. It is not a requirement that wins God's favor or causes you to earn His blessings. He favors us now because we are in Christ. He has already blessed us with every blessing that there is.

"As His divine power has given unto us all things that pertain to life and godliness, through the knowledge of Him who called us by glory and virtue" (2 Peter 1:3).

"Blessed be the God and Father of our Lord Jesus Christ, who has blessed us with every spiritual blessing in Christ" (Eph.1:3).

Prayer is a heavenly partnership with God to advance His kingdom in the earth. It is an invitation to stand with Him in the courts of glory and work alongside Him in accomplishing His will. It is a place of power that He has given us where we reign with Him. Prayer is not just something that we do for God. God, Himself, is a prayer warrior! The scripture tells us that Jesus lives at the right hand of the Father and is praying for us.

"Who is He who condemns? It is Christ who died, and furthermore is risen, who is even at the right hand of God, who also makes intercession for us" (Rom. 8:34).

There is a grace, a supernatural power, in which are to pray. We are not to pray in our own strength. We are to pray in His strength. Because He has called us into such a place of power and privilege, we must be good stewards of this gift. He gives us grace to pray, and we must not receive this grace in vain.

When you pray, you must continue until you are done. What good would it be to start something and not finish? Would a runner begin a race and not finish? Would a great chef cook a meal, only to cook it half done? We must complete the tasks that we have in this great partnership called prayer.

So one may ask, "How do I know when I'm done? How long do I need to pray?" The answer is simple, but not for people who try to pray without the communion of the Holy Spirit. When you pray with an eye on the Holy Spirit, and an ear to His heart, you will know when you have completed a prayer task. You will sense His joy. You will sense His victory and you must stay with it until you do sense that joy and victory.

Often times when praying and interceding, you will sense urgency. You will sense the pain and struggle of those you are praying for. You will pray in the understanding and pray in other tongues while sensing the heart of the Holy Spirit to bring people into victory. You will sense the compassion of the Father for those for whom you pray. While praying and sensing these things, stay with it! Stay with it until you sense His victory.

Many times that victory will come and you will feel like shouting or singing for joy. Sometimes you will have the sense of paddling down a river filled with rapid and dangerous waters, and then all of a sudden the waters change to calm, still waters. A peace begins to take over you. That's when you know you are done, and you must stay with it until you are done.

The scripture tells us to watch and pray. What does that mean? How does a person pray and watch at the same time? What do you watch for when you pray? You watch for signals from the Holy Ghost. He is co-laboring with you and He is the specialist! When you are working with a specialist, you should always keep an eye on Him while you are working. Watch for His cues. Listen for His leading. Follow His promoting, and stay with it until you are done. He will let you know!

Pray in Faith

We should not be people who marvel when our prayers get answered. It shouldn't surprise us when we see something that we prayed about turn around miraculously. If we are praying in faith, then there should be a confidence before, during, and after we pray. We should always expect every prayer to come to pass and we should always expect the power of God to move in situation about which we have prayer.

Jesus came to Peter one day and told him some news that might startle most Christians if they received the same news. He told Peter that Satan was desiring to sift him like wheat. This was not good news to Peter, until Jesus told Peter what He was going to do about it.

And the Lord said, "Simon, Simon! Indeed, Satan has asked for you, that he may sift you as wheat. But I have prayed for you, that your faith should not fail; and when you have returned to Me, strengthen your brethren."

Luke 22:31–32

Jesus had faith that His prayers would come to pass. He was confident. He knew that His prayer was more powerful than the plans of the enemy. He didn't tell Peter, "Now Peter, the devil is going to try and kill you, so you need to be alert and be very careful!" No, He basically told Peter everything was going to be okay because *I prayed!*

We need to have that kind of confidence when we have prayed and received that same note of victory from the Holy Spirit. When you have faith, you must let that faith govern your words, your thoughts and your actions. Prayer people aren't sad people, worried people or anxious people...Prayer people are faith people, and faith shouts and rejoices before the situations change. People of prayer don't marvel when they see the answer come to pass...they expect it to come to pass!

Peter was therefore kept in prison, but constant prayer was offered to God for him by the church. And when Herod was about to bring him out, that night Peter was sleeping, bound with two chains be-

tween two soldiers; and the guards before the door were keeping the prison. Now behold, an angel of the Lord stood by him, and a light shone in the prison; and he struck Peter on the side and raised him up, saying, *"Arise quickly!" And his chains fell off his hands.* Then the angel said to him, *"Gird yourself and tie on your sandals"; and so he did. And he said to him, "Put on your garment and follow me." So he went out and followed him, and did not know that what was done by the angel was real, but thought he was seeing a vision.* When they were past the first and the second guard posts, they came to the iron gate that leads to the city, which opened to them of its own accord; and they went out and went down one street, and immediately the angel departed from him. And when Peter had come to himself, he said, *"Now I know for certain that the Lord has sent His angel, and has delivered me from the hand of Herod and from all the expectation of the Jewish people." So, when he had considered this, he came to the house of Mary, the mother of John whose surname was Mark, where many were gathered together praying. And as Peter knocked at the door of the gate, a girl named Rhoda came to answer. When she recognized*

Peter's voice, because of her gladness she did not open the gate, but ran in and announced that Peter stood before the gate. But they said to her, "You are beside yourself!" Yet she kept insisting that it was so. So they said, "It is his angel." Now Peter continued knocking; and when they opened the door and saw him, they were astonished.

Acts 12:5–16

Here is a story of people praying, but the answer to their prayer shocked them. They were praying for Peter's deliverance, but marveled when He was delivered. We should always be thankful when we see answered prayer, but we shouldn't be surprised or shocked when answered prayer happens. There should be a confidence that what we have prayed *will* come to pass!

Now this is the confidence that we have in Him, that if we ask anything according to His will, He hears us. And if we know that He hears us, whatever we ask, we know that we have the petitions that we have asked of Him.

1 John 5:14–15

Pray With Joy

"I thank my God upon every remembrance of you, 4 always in every prayer of mine making request for you all with joy" (Phil.1:3–4).

If you pray in faith, you will always pray with joy! Why? Because faith always rejoices! Faith sees the end from the beginning. Faith sees though walls that may stand in front of us, and sees victory on the other side. Real faith doesn't wait until it sees the answer to get happy, it gets happy now, before anything may change in the natural realm. Like the children of Israel standing before the walls of Jericho, we march according to God's orders and we shout before the walls come down!

There are two signs that will always tell you if you have faith. Think of it like a road on which you are traveling on. How do you know if you are on the right road? Signs will show up as you are driving. There are two signs that keep showing up when you are on the road of faith. Those signs are *joy* and *peace*.

"Now may the God of hope fill you with all joy and peace in believing, that you may abound in hope by the power of the Holy Spirit" (Rom. 15:13).

Joy and peace are a result of believing. When you believe God's promises it fills you with joy and peace. If joy and peace aren't the signs you are seeing when you pray, then you aren't praying in faith. When we pray, we believe what God has said to us. We believe what we have prayed. We believe that God is faithful to do what He said He will do.

When we pray in other tongues, we believe we have prayed out God's mysteries. We believe we have charged up our internal battery and we believe we are edified. If we do believe, then joy will flow out of our innermost being.

Pray With Thanksgiving!

> *Be anxious for nothing, but in everything by prayer and supplication, with thanksgiving, let your requests be made known to God; and the peace of God, which surpasses all understanding, will guard your hearts and minds through Christ Jesus.*

> **Philippians 4:6–7**

Thanksgiving is an integral part of prayer. If I told you I was going to do something great for you tomorrow, the correct response would be to thank me for what I said I would do. You wouldn't wait until I performed the task. If you believe me to be a man of my word, then you would thank me at the moment that I told you what I would do for you.

When we pray, we are taking God's words and His promises and we are declaring things that He already told us that He would do. We pray with thanksgiving. Once we have prayed and stood on His promise, there remains nothing else to do but to praise Him and be thankful. Thanksgiving is the language of faith!

"Continue earnestly in prayer, being vigilant in it with thanksgiving" (Col. 4:2).

In Conclusion

We cannot just be people who pray, we must be people who stand right and pray! We have been made the righteousness of God in Jesus so we can stand in His presence as if sin never existed. We have been made righteous so we can fellowship with Him. We have been made righteous so we can be effective ambassadors of His. We have been made righteous so we can pray effectively and powerfully.

Take your place in this work of advancing His kingdom all over the earth. You can see powerful transformation in your own life and in the lives of those around you. You can push back and stop the evil plans of the enemy with your prayers. Your God-given authority will be released and things will begin to change. As you stand right and pray, your prayers will be life-transforming and nation-shaking!

"The earnest (heartfelt, continued) prayer of a righteous man makes tremendous power available [dynamic in its working]" (James 5:16b AMP).

ENDNOTES

All scripture in this book, unless otherwise noted, is taken from the New King James Version of the Bible.

ABOUT THE AUTHOR

Dayne Massey ministers with an apostolic anointing, and has stood in the office of pastor and teacher for over thirty years. He has a passion to bring people into a solid understanding of who they are in Christ, teaching them to take a strong place in prayer and in effective ministry. Over the past decade, Dayne has been involved in international Bible schools, training men and women who are preparing for ministry.

Dayne is a 1988 graduate of Rhema Bible College in Tulsa, Oklahoma. He is married to his wife, Lisa and they have one daughter, Lydia. After pastoring for many years, Dayne presently travels extensively in ministry in the USA and internationally, with a passion to see the gospel preached and demonstrated in signs, wonders and miracles. The Masseys are actively involved in equipping believers that reside in nations that are hostile to the gospel through getting discipleship material, like *Stand Right and Pray*, translated and published in these nations.

Along with publishing other books by various authors, *Stand Right and Pray* is presently being published by Dayne Massey Ministries in seven different languages: English, Farsi/Persian, Arabic, Armenian, Western Armenian, Turkish, and Russian. Dayne has also authored a devotional book called *From Servants to Sons*, available in digital format through Amazon and the iTunes bookstore.